CHAMPIONS OF MEN'S SOCCER

CHAM

Also by Ann Killion

CHAMPIONS OF WOMEN'S SOCCER

PIONS
OF
MEN'S
SOCCER

ANN KILLION

PHILOMEL BOOKS

PHILOMEL BOOKS
an imprint of Penguin Random House LLC
375 Hudson Street
New York, NY 10014

Library of Congress Cataloging-in-Publication Data
Names: Killion, Ann, author.
Title: Champions of men's soccer / Ann Killion.
Description: New York : Philomel Books, [2018] | Audience: Ages: 8–12.
| Audience: Grades: 4 to 6. | Identifiers: LCCN 2017041798 | ISBN
9780399548987 (hardcover) | ISBN 9780399548994 (ebook)
Subjects: LCSH: Soccer players—Biography—Juvenile literature. |
Soccer players—Rating of—Juvenile literature.
Classification: LCC GV942.7.A1 K54 2018 | DDC 796.3340922 [B]—dc23
LC record available at https://lccn.loc.gov/2017041798
Printed in the United States of America.
ISBN 9780399548987
10 9 8 7 6 5 4 3 2 1

Edited by Brian Geffen.
Design by Ellice M. Lee.
Text set in 11.5-pt Book Antiqua.

For my champion, Connor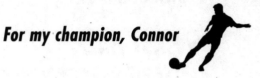

CONTENTS

▶ **PREGAME**   IX
INTRODUCTION

▶ **FIRST HALF**   9
THE INTERNATIONAL STARTING 11
Pelé
Lionel Messi
Diego Maradona
Cristiano Ronaldo
Franz Beckenbauer
Xavi
Johan Cruyff
Zinedine Zidane
Ronaldo
Paolo Maldini
Gianluigi Buffon

▶ **HALFTIME**   101
LEAGUES AROUND THE WORLD

▶ **SECOND HALF**   117
THE AMERICAN STARTING 11

Landon Donovan

Tim Howard

Joe Gaetjens

Claudio Reyna

Eric Wynalda

Clint Dempsey

Michael Bradley

Jozy Altidore

Brad Friedel

Paul Caligiuri

Christian Pulisic

▶ **EXTRA TIME**   **215**
WORLD CUP HIGHLIGHTS

▶ **PENALTY KICKS**   **251**
THE NEXT GENERATION OF SUPERSTARS

▶ **PHOTOS**   **269**

▶ **INDEX**   **277**

►►► **PREGAME**

INTRODUCTION

People like to debate all sorts of things about sports. Who's the best player? What's the hardest game to master? But there's no debate about this:

The most popular sport in the world is soccer.

Or as most of the rest of the world calls it, "football."

You might not believe that fact if you live in the United States. From watching TV or listening to local fans talk about their favorite sports, you would think (American) football or basketball is the most popular sport in the universe.

But every four years, when the World Cup is played, Americans get a dose of reality. And they realize that, *nope*, soccer is by far the sport that the rest of the world loves best. Unfortunately for the United States, in 2018 they won't attend the World Cup party.

To put the sport's fan base in perspective, the

final of the 2014 World Cup between Germany and Argentina was watched by an estimated one billion people. That's one seventh of the world's population. In contrast, the audience for Super Bowl LI in February 2017 between New England and Atlanta was 111 million.

Not even close.

According to FIFA, the international governing body of the sport, about 265 million people worldwide play organized soccer in some form or another. That's about 4 percent of the world's entire population.

Soccer is played in virtually every corner of the planet, on every continent (even Antarctica!), among people of every economic group and ethnicity.

The primary reason for soccer's immense popularity is its simplicity. It can be played anywhere: on a field, in a street, on a beach. It requires virtually no equipment, save for a ball. And when even a ball isn't available or affordable, one can be made of balled-up rags—as the famous Pelé played with as a child—or other material. Two rocks, or shoes, or lines in the dirt can make up the goal. Kids play barefoot or in sneakers if they don't have cleats. In fact, all you really need to play is passion, determination, and some odds and ends.

Some people complain about soccer's low scores. But the fact that a game is often won by just one goal highlights the competitive tension and also makes for many upsets, one of the most compelling things about any sport.

Another reason for soccer's popularity is the fact that it's been around for centuries, perhaps millennia. There is evidence that some form of the sport was played as long as three thousand years ago. There was an early form of the game called *cuju* in China in the third century BC. Precursors of the game were played in ancient Greece and ancient Rome. Many people believe the Romans spread a form of the game throughout Europe, with the expansion of the Roman Empire, including to England. There are even stories of early versions of the game played by mobs of people, which quickly transformed into riots, therefore leading to the game being outlawed.

Fast-forward to England in the nineteenth century. The game was played at schools, including Rugby School and Eton College, which played two different versions, one where the ball could be picked up (at

Rugby) and one where it was played with only the feet (at Eton). One became the game of rugby and the other became football, or soccer.

As the years went on and soccer grew in popularity, the sport's guidelines became more official. In 1848, players at Cambridge drew up a set of formal rules for the game. The first international game was played in 1872, between England and Scotland. England went on to export the game to its colonies throughout the British Empire.

The first official soccer organization, the FA (Football Association), was formed at the Freemasons' Tavern in London in 1863 with twelve football clubs. Then in 1904, FIFA—the Fédération Internationale de Football Association—was founded; the original members were Belgium, Denmark, France, the Netherlands, Spain, Sweden, and Switzerland. England joined a year later. Within three decades, FIFA had grown its membership to forty-one nations.

The organized game spread throughout the world, carried across oceans by Europeans to countries where they had a presence, through colonization or business.

The most notable exception was North America. The United States (and Canada) seemed impervious to the charms of organized soccer for a century. Despite America's English roots and even though the United States is a nation built on immigrants, soccer took a long time to catch on.

Why?

It's difficult to say for sure, but we can make a few educated guesses. First, by the time soccer was expanding across the world, there were already two very popular sports in the United States: baseball and (American) football. Baseball was the country's first professional sport. Football, which was an evolution of rugby, was established through the growing collegiate system. Some historians believe there just wasn't enough room for another major sport in America, especially a hundred years ago when people had less leisure time to spend either playing or watching sports.

In addition, the United States has always valued being unique and different from European countries. Despite America's English roots, our country's story is that we defeated the English in the American Revolution. So it's not surprising that our country might reject a sport so very British at its core, when America had its own unique sports to play.

America even has its own name for the game.

Though the term *soccer* originated in England—as a shortened version of *association football* to distinguish it from *rugby football*—it only later became popularized in the United States. The name *soccer* kept the sport separate from American football, which became just *football* in America. The term *soccer* is also used in other countries that have another prevalent form of football, such as Australia.

Even though it wasn't the most important sport like it was in other countries, soccer still gained a foothold in the United States. As different waves of immigrants arrived during the twentieth century, they brought the game they loved with them and taught it to their children. Youth soccer—among both boys and girls—grew quickly during the second half of the twentieth century.

And when the United States hosted the 1994 World Cup—a strategic move by FIFA to grow the game in such a large and rich country—soccer really began to take off. America was about a century behind the rest of the world, but by the late twentieth century there was room in the United States for interest in a variety of sports.

Now, after decades of effort, the world's most

popular sport is also one of the most popular sports in America. Our national teams are hugely popular, the World Cup gets big television ratings, there is an established professional league in Major League Soccer, and, thanks to cable television and live streaming, fans have access to games from the best leagues around the world. Though there is concern that missing the World Cup in 2018 will set the sport back in the United States, it is still here to stay.

In this book, we will look at what makes men's soccer the most popular and thrilling sport in the world (there's also a *Champions of Women's Soccer* book specifically about the women's game).

From the near-mythological players of the past to the greats of today, we will look at the most important superstars in the world and the most important American players—not necessarily the best players but the ones who have had a key impact on the game. We will journey back in time to the most important moments in the history of the game and also explore some of the top leagues in the world. Finally, we will look to the future and explore some of the young players who could emerge as the next generation of stars.

Maybe you won't agree with all my picks—maybe

you have your own lists. But that's one of the most fun things about sports: arguing about who is the best. Everyone has an opinion, and we could debate about sports until the end of time.

But one thing's for sure: the world's most popular sport is going to be around a long time.

► ► ► **FIRST HALF**

THE INTERNATIONAL STARTING 11

PELÉ

What's the greatest goal? The greatest game? The best World Cup?

Those are all soccer questions open to debate. This one isn't:

Who's the greatest soccer player ever?

The answer is Pelé.

Even almost half a century after he last played in a World Cup, even with all the fabulous soccer talent on the planet right now, Pelé remains the acknowledged greatest player ever.

"I sometimes feel as though [soccer] was invented for this magical player," said Sir Bobby Charlton, an English midfielder who competed against Pelé during his career.

Pelé's is one of those rags-to-riches stories that make soccer so fascinating. He was born Edson Arantes do Nascimento in 1940 in Brazil. He was named after Thomas Edison, the inventor of the first commercially successful electric lightbulb. The name proved to be fitting—though Pelé wasn't a scientist, he was definitely an innovator and ended up generating electricity worldwide.

The greatest player in the world grew up in poverty in Bauru, Brazil, in the state of São Paulo, playing soccer on the streets with a sock stuffed with rags or even a grapefruit since he couldn't afford a real ball. His father was a semiprofessional soccer player but did not succeed at the professional level and struggled financially, working as a janitor. Pelé never played with a real, leather ball until he was a teenager. Though his family called him "Dico"—a pet name his uncle bestowed—somewhere along the way he acquired the nickname "Pelé", which he originally hated. He thought it sounded bad.

He was discovered by Waldemar de Brito, a former member of the Brazilian national team, who was his youth coach. De Brito persuaded Pelé's family to let him try out for the club Santos when he was fifteen. Soon he was a team regular, far from home and sleeping on bunks in the team stadium with other young players. He led the team in goals in his first full season.

By the time he was seventeen, Pelé was on the Brazilian national team. He played in his first World Cup, in Sweden in 1958, before his eighteenth birthday, becoming the youngest player ever to play in a World Cup. He didn't play in the tournament's first two games, partly because of a knee injury, but his teammates convinced the coach to start him in the third.

That World Cup in Sweden was when the rest of the world got a glimpse of the man who would become the most famous soccer player—and arguably the most famous athlete for a time—on Earth. He was a sensation. His speed and vision were breathtaking. He could score with either foot. He was elusive and clever and played with an unabashed joy.

"The head talks to the heart," Pelé once said, describing how he played, "and the heart talks to the feet."

Brazilians call soccer the "jogo bonito"—the beautiful game. Pelé helped popularize the term, not only by using it to describe his game but also to characterize the way he played. He played a distinctly Brazilian type of soccer, with pure joy and the rhythm of a samba, a traditional form of music and dance popular in his country.

In the semifinal of the 1958 World Cup, Pelé scored three goals—a hat trick—in a 5–2 win over France, becoming the youngest player ever to do so in a World Cup. His scoring spree didn't end there. He scored two more goals in a 5–2 win over host Sweden in the final, on the way to helping his country bring home the championship.

Pelé had been motivated to win a World Cup ever since he was nine and Brazil had lost to Uruguay in the final in Rio de Janeiro. That day he promised his father he would win a World Cup. When he won his first in Sweden, he wept with joy. It was the first World Cup victory for Brazil, which would eventually lead all countries with five.

Brazil won its first World Cup just as television was gaining popularity. That helped his fame spread quickly around the world. Brazil's team was also racially mixed, which made it distinct from those of many of the other world powers. Pelé became an inspiration to people of color around the world.

After the 1958 World Cup, Pelé was sought after by many of the top European clubs. But the government of Brazil proclaimed him "a national treasure," to prevent him from being signed elsewhere, and his club team, Santos, held on to Pelé. The club became the first globe-trotting soccer team, scheduling matches around the world so that other soccer fans could see the great Pelé. Once, in an exhibition in Nigeria, a cease-fire in a civil war was called to allow both sides to watch Pelé play soccer.

Let that sink in. Pelé was so exciting to watch, he caused a country to decide to pause a war.

Pelé led Santos to great success. The club won eight titles and six Brazilian national championships, including five in a row, from 1961 to 1965. In 1962 and 1963 it won the Copa Libertadores and went on to win the Intercontinental Cup. It was considered one of the greatest club teams ever assembled.

Meanwhile, after his first successful international campaign, Pelé led Brazil back to the 1962 World Cup in Chile. Though he suffered a groin injury, which sidelined him for all but two games, Brazil won a second-straight world title. Four years later, in England in 1966, Pelé again was injured—due to the rough tactics of defenders—and Brazil lost to Portugal. Pelé was so frustrated afterward that he said he would never play in another World Cup.

But he changed his mind, and that decision helped

cement his legend even further. In 1970, in the World Cup in Mexico, Brazil came roaring back on the world stage. Considered one of the finest teams ever assembled, Brazil beat rival Uruguay in the semifinals and in the final beat Italy, 4–1. Pelé scored four goals in his World Cup farewell tournament and was named the player of the tournament. He is the only player to have been part of three world championships.

Pelé retired from Santos in 1974. But a year later, he shocked the soccer world by coming out of retirement to play for the New York Cosmos, a team in the North American Soccer League (NASL), a league that had little impact and was almost dead before his arrival.

His presence helped make the league a huge attraction. For many Americans, it was their first introduction to soccer. The three-year, $2.8 million contract made Pelé the highest-paid athlete in the world. Ten million people tuned in to watch his debut with the Cosmos. He drew huge crowds everywhere he played. Though he was thirty-four years old when he joined the team, far past his prime, Pelé was still the main attraction and an impressive goal scorer. And his presence brought other players to the NASL—the great

German player Franz Beckenbauer was Pelé's team-mate. Others, like Johan Cruyff and George Best, played for other teams.

Pelé played his final match in October 1977, an exhibition between the Cosmos and his old club Santos. He played a half for each team. The NASL folded seven years later, and it was more than a decade before a truly successful soccer league was launched in the United States.

Pelé won several awards as the best athlete of the twentieth century. He received honorary British knighthood and served as an ambassador to the United Nations.

Though Diego Maradona's fans would argue that their player was the best ever, and the debate about Lionel Messi and Cristiano Ronaldo can be heated, Pelé's legend is set in stone.

His bookended World Cups—one coming when he was seventeen and the other coming in 1970 when he was already a global superstar—will be hard for another player to ever match. His peers were quick to acknowledge that he was the greatest player they had ever played against.

There have been so many great players in the

game. But there's very little argument over who is the greatest of all time.

Pelé.

STATISTICS:

Position: forward

Appearances for Brazilian national team: 92

Goals for Brazil: 77

Professional appearances (two clubs): 694

Goals for professional clubs: 650

LIONEL MESSI

Too small, the naysayers said. Obviously, way too small.

How can such a tiny boy play soccer in his own age group? Forget playing professionally. Forget playing for his country. Forget being one of the greatest players to ever play the game.

But as it turned out, Lionel Messi wasn't too small. He overcame the doubts to become perhaps the greatest soccer player of the modern era. An astonishing goal scorer, he captivated fans around the world.

And he also offered inspiration to anyone who has ever been told that they couldn't do something.

"He's well above anything else I've ever seen," said his former Barca teammate Carles Puyol. "He's an alien."

In truth, Messi was born on planet Earth in Rosario, Argentina, in 1987, one year after undersized legend

Diego Maradona had won a World Cup for Argentina. At the time, Argentinians didn't think they'd ever see another native player as great. But they were wrong.

As a young boy growing up, Messi was part of a soccer-crazy family. He played with his father, his older brothers, and two cousins who went on to professional careers. He was quick, balanced, and skilled; had amazing ball control; and was an unbelievable scoring machine. Between ages six and twelve, Messi scored five hundred goals for his Newell's Old Boys team.

But as his teammates grew, Messi didn't. When he was eleven years old, he was just four feet, two inches tall. That was when doctors discovered that he had a growth hormone deficiency and needed treatment. Every day, for three years, he had to take a shot.

"I was always the smallest of them all," Messi said. "It was like this until I finished the treatment, and then I started to grow properly."

Though human growth hormone is controversial because some athletes have used it to an unfair advantage as adults, it has long been used in the treatment of children with growth deficiencies.

The treatment worked for Messi, but it was very

expensive. His parents both worked in manufacturing factories and had trouble paying for the medical expense. His father, Jorge, asked Messi's youth team, the Newell's Old Boys, to help pay for it. Originally the club said it would cover the full cost, but after it gave a small amount, Jorge said he never received any more.

Messi was willing to put shots in his legs as a child, and his parents were willing to pay for it, and his club was willing to consider funding the treatment, because he was so gifted on the soccer field. Even before he started growing, Messi had found a way to use his small size to his advantage.

"I think being smaller than the rest allowed me to be a bit quicker and more agile," he said.

Messi's family had ties to Catalonia, Spain. Those ties led to renowned Spanish club FC Barcelona offering to pay for Messi's treatment, and at thirteen, he had a tryout with the famed team. He was signed immediately and he and his family relocated to Spain and lived in an apartment near Camp Nou.

But the family was unhappy, in particular his younger sister. After a six-month stay, Messi's mother went back to Argentina to live with Messi's three siblings. Jorge stayed in Barcelona with his son. The split was very difficult for the family, and Messi was terribly homesick.

But he stayed. It was a risk for the entire family. Because how many thirteen-year-olds who dream of becoming a professional at the highest level actually achieve that fairy tale?

Messi did.

After playing for the youth academy he enrolled in the Royal Spanish Football Federation and began playing regularly. He became close friends with future greats Cesc Fàbregas and Gerard Piqué, becoming part of a "Baby Dream Team." He received an offer to move to the talented English club Arsenal, but while his good friends left for England, Messi remained committed to Barcelona.

He made his debut with the senior team in 2004, at seventeen, in a friendly against a Portuguese team. Brazilian star Ronaldinho, who had recently joined Barcelona, befriended Messi, called him "little brother," and told people the young player would soon surpass him.

Messi received limited playing time that season, scoring his first goal in May, on an assist from

Ronaldinho. His main task was to put muscle on his small frame, to become a stronger player.

On his eighteenth birthday, Messi signed his first contract with the senior team. He became a starter the next season and also acquired Spanish citizenship. That created a subplot that continued throughout his career: while Spaniards thought of him as Argentinian, many of Messi's own countrymen considered him too Spanish. But despite the fact that Messi was on a Spanish club, he was committed to Argentina and the national team. Though he was informally asked about playing for Spain, he always wanted to represent his own country. He began playing for Argentina's youth teams in 2004.

He debuted with Argentina's senior team in a friendly match in 2005. He was almost immediately sent off for elbowing an opponent. A month later he played in a World Cup qualifier. In the 2006 World Cup in Germany, he was a substitute for most of the competition. However, he didn't get on the field in his team's quarterfinal loss to host Germany, and many criticized Argentina's coach for that decision.

Messi continue to play with Argentina, sometimes over Barcelona's objections. In 2008, he wanted to play for Argentina's U-23 team at the Beijing Olympics, which conflicted with Barcelona's Champions League qualifiers. He was finally allowed to play and his team won the gold medal, beating Nigeria in the championship game; he assisted on the game's only goal and tormented the Nigerian defense.

Messi's brilliance began to truly reveal itself when he was in his early twenties. Because of his small stature, he had a knack for slipping between defenders, evading tackles, and changing direction. He is predominantly left-footed and considered the best dribbler in the world; his former manager, Pep Guardiola, said Messi was the only player he's ever seen who was faster dribbling the ball than running without it. He always seems to be going forward to the goal, perfectly balanced and drawing all defenders. A typical Messi goal comes off beating a defender with his quickness and then unleashing a powerful, perfectly placed shot that leaves the goalkeeper helpless.

As Messi evolved into arguably the best player in the world with Barcelona, he led his club to several La Liga titles and four Champions League titles, and he earned the Ballon d'Or as best player in the world a record five times from 2009 to 2016. He is often directly compared to Cristiano Ronaldo—the two traded the Ballon d'Or award back and forth for a decade, with the other usually finishing as the runner-up. The stars were direct competitors in La Liga and also were frequently compared in terms of salary, popularity, and endorsements.

If you asked ten soccer fans who the best player in the world was, you'd get five votes for Messi and five for Ronaldo.

Though Messi succeeded impressively with his club, he has not been able to achieve the same level of success with Argentina. Prior to the 2010 World Cup in Germany, under coach Diego Maradona, Argentina struggled to qualify for the World Cup. Though the team made it to Germany, its woeful defense was a problem. Germany destroyed Argentina 4-0 in the quarterfinals.

By 2011, Messi had assumed the captaincy of the national team. In the 2014 World Cup, Argentina had more success, advancing to the finals before losing the championship 1-0 in extra time to Germany. Though Messi won the Golden Ball as best player of the tournament, both he—and that choice—received some criticism because he was unable to score in the knockout rounds.

Argentina could never field a complete team

around the brilliant goal scorer. Messi's frustrations continued after the World Cup. In 2015, Argentina made it to the final of the Copa América but lost in penalty kicks to host Chile. The next year, the hundredth anniversary of the Copa América was contested in the United States. Messi, though suffering a back injury, was electric—scoring five goals and notching four assists—and led Argentina to the finals.

However, the team lost again on penalty kicks to Chile, and after the game, in which he missed his own penalty kick, Messi announced he was retiring from international play at age twenty-nine. But within a matter of weeks, he unretired and was included in his country's World Cup qualifiers. In one of his finest moments, Messi scored three goals on the final day of qualifying to put Argentina into the 2018 World Cup.

In 2017, Messi signed a new contract with Barcelona that should keep him with the club through 2021. Despite that seeming security, rumors swirled around Messi's future with the club after Neymar's departure for Paris Saint-Germain (PSG) announced a changing era for the team.

Though his club was changing, Messi remained the gold standard for players.

"Messi is the best I've ever seen," said Roy Keane, a former Manchester United player. "I don't dish out praise lightly, but Messi deserves it. I look for weaknesses in his game and I can't find them."

The best ever? Messi has been making the argument for years. And proving that he was never too small for his big dreams.

STATISTICS*:

Position: forward

Appearances for Argentinean national team: 118

Goals for Argentina: 58

Appearances for Barcelona: 387

Goals for Barcelona: 358

*currently active player

DIEGO MARADONA

One of the most talented players ever came in a five-foot-five package of whirling energy, hot temper, constant controversy, and otherworldly skill.

Diego Maradona is the greatest player to ever play for Argentina. Though Lionel Messi has given Maradona a strong challenge, until Messi leads his team to a World Cup championship, he won't be able to unseat Maradona in the legend of Argentinian soccer.

Maradona was also considered the greatest player of the 1980s, a period when—thanks to huge strides in television coverage—more people around the globe had an opportunity to watch him play. Before long, legions of fans around the world were wearing the distinct blue-and-white-vertical-striped jerseys of Argentina, emblazoned with Maradona's famed No. 10.

Maradona was born in 1960 in Buenos Aires and

grew up in very poor circumstances. But it wasn't long before his talent was recognized. He was only eight years old when he was spotted by the coach of a youth team called Los Cebollitas (the Little Onions) and was invited to join. That team won 136 consecutive games and a national championship.

He made his first division club debut a few days before his sixteenth birthday, and four months later he played his first game with the national team, becoming the youngest to ever play for Argentina.

In 1978, Argentina hosted the World Cup, but Maradona couldn't play because the national team coach decided he was too young, at only seventeen. That Argentina team won the World Cup, the first championship for its country. But the country's best player was still waiting in the wings: Maradona led his under-20 squad to a Junior World Cup championship and was dubbed the star of the tournament, winning the Golden Ball. The skill he displayed in his compact body and dazzling left foot was unmatched, dancing around defenders, never losing possession.

While Maradona waited to play in a World Cup, his professional career was on the fast track. He played with the Argentinos Juniors for five seasons, scoring 115 goals in 167 appearances, and then signed a contract with Argentina's most famous team, Boca Juniors, at twenty. As a member of the team, Maradona argued often with his manager, Silvio Marzolini. Still, Maradona and his teammates managed to win the league title that year, but his contentious relationship with his manager was one of the first of many controversial moments to come.

One year later, the 1982 World Cup took place in Spain, and coincidentally, Maradona was already rumored to be headed to the host country to live there full-time. For a record-setting fee of $7.6 million, after just one season, he was transferred from Boca Juniors to Barcelona.

Before he would step onto the field for Barcelona, though, Maradona played in his first World Cup. In Argentina's opening game, held at Barcelona's famous Camp Nou stadium, Maradona was treated as a savior by the local fans. But in his first game in his new home stadium, Argentina lost to Belgium 1–0.

The team advanced out of the first round, but that was a strange World Cup format with a double knock-out round. Argentina lost both those games, first to Brazil—in a game where Maradona was sent off after receiving a red card for a high kick—and then to eventual champion Italy.

The rough start at the Spain World Cup foreshadowed Maradona's difficult time in Spain with FC Barcelona. Despite the fact that he scored forty-five goals in seventy-three games, his tenure at Camp Nou is most remembered for injury, illness, fights, and tension with his bosses. In one memorable match against rival Real Madrid, he was the main protagonist in a brawl on the field. In 1984, he again broke the transfer fee record, this time moving to Napoli in Italy's Serie A for $10.48 million.

He was again welcomed as a conquering hero in Napoli, a team that was often overshadowed by the teams in the north of Italy. Maradona was a scoring machine, and he eventually led Napoli to two Italian championships, the first ever in the club's history.

Maradona's greatest moment came at the 1986 World Cup in Mexico. Wearing the captain's armband, he scored five goals, including two in a quarterfinal against England that are among the most famous goals in history. First, Maradona brought the ball downfield, passed to a teammate on his right, and ran toward goal as the English goalkeeper came out. Maradona received the ball with his head, his arm raised high, and hit it into the net! England's players immediately called for a handball, but there was no whistle. Replays clearly showed that the ball did go off his hand and the goal became known as "The Hand of God."

His second goal in that game isn't as famous but was far more beautiful. He received the ball at midfield and danced through the English defenders, as though the ball were invisibly connected to his foot, past the charging goalkeeper, and finished by flicking the ball into the net. The goal was voted "Goal of the Century" in one FIFA poll.

"When Diego scored that second goal against us, I felt like applauding," said English striker Gary Lineker. "It was impossible to score such a beautiful goal."

Maradona scored another pair of goals against Belgium in the semifinal, and Argentina defeated West Germany in the championship match to win its second World Cup. Maradona was awarded the Golden Ball for his incredible performance throughout the tournament.

In the 1990 World Cup in Italy, Maradona, playing with an ankle injury, was not the force he had been four years earlier. With their captain playing at half speed, Argentina lacked their usual dominance. They were almost eliminated in the first round. Yet Argentina still advanced to the final, defeating both Yugoslavia in the quarterfinals and host Italy in the semifinals on penalty kicks. But the team fell to West Germany 1–0 in the final.

Maradona seemed to attract success and failure in equal measure. In his thirties, Maradona continued to be controversial. His career in Napoli ended after he failed a drug test and he was said to be addicted to cocaine. Because of his addiction, his performance on the field suffered. He moved to Seville for one year and then back to Argentina, where he played three more seasons—two with the Boca Juniors—before retiring.

His final World Cup appearance also ended in disgrace. At the 1994 World Cup, he played in just two games before he was sent home from the United States after testing positive for a banned substance.

After his playing career was over, Maradona tried his hand at managing. He was named the head coach of the Argentinian team in the 2010 World Cup, but the team struggled to qualify despite the talent of star forward Lionel Messi. In South Africa, Argentina made it through to the quarterfinals but was crushed by Germany 4-0, and Messi was viewed as a disappointment. As with so much of his career, Maradona flashed his temper and battled with the press. His contract was not renewed.

With the rise of Messi as another world superstar, there is frequently debate about who is the better player. But the legions of Argentina fans who continue to sing a song in Spanish that claims "Maradona is better than Pelé"—more than a decade after their hero retired—still believe that Maradona is the greatest Argentinian player ever and one of the greatest to ever play the game.

STATISTICS:

Position: attacking midfielder/striker

Appearances for Argentinean national team: 91

Goals for Argentina: 35

Professional appearances (seven clubs): 491

Goals for professional clubs: 259

CRISTIANO RONALDO

For many years, soccer fans were obsessed with the debate about who was the better player: Pelé or Diego Maradona?

In recent years, the argument has shifted: Who is better, Cristiano Ronaldo or Lionel Messi?

Unlike Pelé vs. Maradona, who played in different eras and leagues, the Ronaldo vs. Messi debate had the added element of an intense team rivalry. Ronaldo and Messi are two of the greatest players ever, going head to head in one of soccer's greatest rivalries, between Real Madrid and Barcelona.

For a time early in his career, Cristiano Ronaldo was considered only the second-best "Ronaldo" in soccer. He shared part of the same name as the Brazilian forward, who was considered the best player in the world for a time. But Cristiano surpassed not only the other Ronaldo but also almost all of the other players in the world.

"He has magic in his boots," said Eusébio, a Portuguese soccer legend, of Ronaldo. "He believes he can do anything with the ball, and that confidence makes him very special indeed."

Cristiano Ronaldo dos Santos Aveiro was born in 1985 on the Portuguese island of Madeira, the youngest of four children. He was given his second name in honor of Ronald Reagan, who was president of the United States at the time. He grew up around the soccer field—his father was the equipment manager for the local club, Andorinha. Ronaldo played for that club's youth program and later with another team, Nacional. When he was twelve, he had a tryout with Sporting CP, in the Portuguese capital of Lisbon, and the team signed him.

But soon after he started down the path to making his dream come true, as a teenager, Ronaldo's soccer career was threatened by an irregular heartbeat. When he played, his heart would race. He had an operation in which a laser was used to cauterize the source of the problem, and he returned to practice a few days later. Though the teenager wasn't too worried about his health issue, his mother was terribly frightened and concerned he might never play again.

She needn't have worried. Ronaldo quickly rose through the youth ranks of Sporting CP and made his debut on the first team at age sixteen. Ronaldo had grown into a tall—six-foot, one-inch—player with speed, grace, and mesmerizing ball skill.

His talents blossomed so much during the 2002–2003 season that he quickly drew the attention of some of the major clubs in Europe. He was noticed by Sir Alex Ferguson, the manager of celebrated English club Manchester United, when Sporting defeated Man U in an exhibition match in Lisbon. The Manchester players urged their boss to sign the young prodigy. At eighteen, Ronaldo signed with Manchester United, and his transfer fee—about $15 million—was at the time the most ever for a teenager in English history.

Playing forward for one of the most high-profile teams in the world, Ronaldo catapulted to stardom. He played with Manchester United for six seasons, appearing in 196 games and scoring eighty-four goals. Along the way, he helped his club win three Premier League titles and the Champions League title. In 2008 Ronaldo was named the FIFA World Player of the Year and winner of the Ballon d'Or.

In 2009, Ronaldo joined Real Madrid for a transfer

fee that set a world record: about $131 million. The move captivated the soccer world at the time, with emotions running high on both sides; at one point Man U filed a tampering complaint, which was dismissed.

The move created a dynamic rivalry with Messi, considered the best player at the time. Suddenly, the two superstars were rival players on historic rival La Liga teams—Ronaldo with Real Madrid and Messi with Barcelona—who seemed intent on trying to best the other on the field with their teams and also in all statistical categories. In 2010–2011, Ronaldo scored the most goals in the history of La Liga; the next year Messi broke that record. From 2008 to 2017, Messi and Ronaldo won the sport's highest award, as FIFA Player of the Year, five times apiece.

"I think we push each other," Ronaldo said of Messi. "This is why the competition is so high."

Ronaldo led Real Madrid to two La Liga titles and three Champions League titles. In 2016, he became the club's all-time leading scorer. By the end of the 2017 season, when Real Madrid again won La Liga and became the first team in history to win consecutive Champions League titles, he had scored an amazing

260 goals in 250 appearances. Though there had been questions earlier in the season about whether his form was slipping, at thirty-two he was the most dominant player in the world. And one of the most popular, with children around the globe wearing his No. 7 jersey and millions following him on social media.

While he was becoming one of the most famous professional players in the world, Ronaldo was also playing for Portugal. He rose quickly through his country's youth teams and in 2004, he played on the U-23 Olympic team in Athens, which finished at the bottom of its group. But the fortunes of the senior national team were better. Ronaldo played his first game with the Portuguese senior team at age eighteen, and the next year he played in the European Championship, which was hosted by his country. Portugal made it to the final but lost 1–0 to a surprising Greece team. Still, teenaged Ronaldo had made his international impression, leading his team into the final, and was clearly a superstar of the future.

In 2006, Ronaldo's team finished fourth at the World Cup, the team's best finish in forty years, since it had finished third in 1966. In a quarterfinal game against England during the tournament, Ronaldo incited controversy by aggressively complaining about a foul by his Manchester United teammate Wayne Rooney. On the international stage, though, the two players were competitors. Rooney received a red card and was sent off, creating some anger toward Ronaldo from his English fans. Portugal ended up losing to France in the semifinal.

In the 2010 World Cup, Portugal lost to eventual champions Spain in the round of 16. Though the early exit was disappointing, it marked a new stage in Ronaldo's international career, as he'd been named team captain for the tournament and was selected as Man of the Match in all three of Portugal's games.

In 2014, Portugal was drawn into a difficult group with Germany, Ghana, and the United States and was unable to advance, due to a 4–0 drubbing by Germany and a 2–2 tie with the Americans. Portugal was a one-man team: Ronaldo was the only true star and teams knew if they controlled him, the Seleção, as the team is called in Portuguese, would not be much of threat.

In the 2016 European Championship, Portugal finally broke through and won its first major championship. Ronaldo was the key player throughout the tournament, scoring three goals to become the all-time leading scorer in the Euros. However, in the final against France, he was injured on a hard challenge and could not keep playing. He was taken off the field on a stretcher. But the team won 1–0 in extra time and Ronaldo finally had guided Portugal to a major title.

"I am very happy," he said afterward. "It is a trophy for all the Portuguese."

Despite his success, at times, Ronaldo has been viewed as a controversial player. Some have called him arrogant and accused the Portuguese captain of flopping on the field to draw fouls. He once said that "people are jealous of me because I am young, handsome and rich," which might have been true but didn't do much to increase his likability.

"I don't mind people hating me because it pushes me," he once said.

In truth, he was immensely popular worldwide, with a huge following on social media and his own CR7 brand. At times, his perfect hairstyle, fashion sense, and underwear ads obscured all the hard work and perfectionism Ronaldo brought to the field. A young, skilled phenom when he first made it onto the international stage, he built himself into a physically commanding, dominating player.

Ronaldo wide on the wing was always a nightmare for defenders, but as he got older and stronger, he began to use his head more, and look to pass. He beat opponents one-on-one, and even late in his career he was still one of the fastest on the field, either with or without the ball at his feet.

Ronaldo was one of the greatest players in the world, playing out one of the great rivalries in sports history and breaking records along the way. The answer to the question of who's better, Ronaldo or Messi, is by no means clear-cut. But between his natural swagger and impressive play on the field, there's no doubt that Ronaldo has emerged as one of the most *popular* athletes in the world. And the 2018 World Cup will be one more chance to see the master at his craft.

STATISTICS*:

Position: forward
Appearances for Portuguese national team: 143
Goals for Portugal: 75

Professional appearances (three clubs): 486
   (Sporting CP 25, Manchester United 196,
   Real Madrid 265)
Goals for professional clubs: 372 (Sporting CP 3,
   Manchester United 84, Real Madrid 285)
*currently active player

FRANZ BECKENBAUER

Franz Beckenbauer was an inspiration for all defenders: he proved that playing on the backline was still a path to superstardom.

Beckenbauer was nicknamed "Der Kaiser," or "The Emperor" in German, because of his leadership skills and commanding play on the field. He is considered the greatest player in German soccer history, though some modern players have given him a challenge. He is one of the greatest athletic heroes Germany has ever known.

He started out as a midfielder but moved back to central defense where he pioneered the position of attacking sweeper, also sometimes called a *libero*. Beckenbauer was free to roam on defense and move into the attack, linking the backline and the midfield, using his vision, pace, and calm to control the game.

"Franz was a marvelous distributor of the ball,

a great tackler, he always had control of the situation and never panicked," said Sir Bobby Charlton, whose England team battled against Beckenbauer. "The most important thing he had was fantastic vision . . . such a hard player to play against."

Beckenbauer was born in Munich in 1945 and grew up in the ruins of post–World War II Germany. He started playing soccer as a child in youth leagues and then joined Bayern Munich as a teenager.

When Beckenbauer was a young boy, when Germany was still divided into two nations, East and West, West Germany's victory in the 1954 World Cup—nicknamed "The Miracle of Bern"—had a huge impact on him. The celebrations gave West Germany, still trying to recover from the ravages of war and the shame of the nation's recent past, a huge psychological lift. Germans used the phrase *"Wir Sind Wieder Wer"* ("We are somebody again"). An inspired nine-year-old Beckenbauer told his parents that he would win a World Cup someday.

Four years later, he joined Bayern Munich—a relationship that would shape much of his life. He made his debut at the senior level in 1964, when he was nineteen. At the time, the team was playing at the regional level. In his first season, he helped Bayern get promoted to the newly formed top-level Bundesliga. Beckenbauer spent the next twelve years of his professional career with Bayern Munich. With Beckenbauer leading the team, they became a force, winning four league championships and three European Cups.

In 1965, at age twenty, Beckenbauer made his debut for West Germany. Less than a year later, he was playing in his first World Cup in England. Though he would make his mark as a defender, he also was an adept scorer, as he proved in 1966. He scored two goals in his debut against Switzerland and four goals in the tournament, where West Germany reached the finals before losing to host England. It was valuable experience that would help shape Beckenbauer's international career.

Four years later, he played in his second World Cup in Mexico. In the semifinal against Italy, Beckenbauer suffered a dislocated shoulder, yet continued playing with his arm in a sling. Now *that* is true dedication. However, Italy beat Germany, which finished third.

With Bayern Munich he had already been experimenting with playing the attacking sweeper role, which he used to potent effect in the 1974 World Cup.

He kept order on the backline, dictated ball control, and kept his team organized and efficient. His style fulfilled stereotypes about the German personality, such as a strong sense of discipline and structure, and it was highly effective.

But despite the stereotype, Beckenbauer was also a creative and elegant player, coming forward and attacking whenever he had the opportunity. His dribbling was silky and mesmerizing. He often unleashed rocket shots from midfield when he had a clear look at the goal.

The 1974 World Cup was held on German soil, and there was pressure from the country to win. Beckenbauer was the captain of the talented team that included Gerd Müeller, the top goal scorer in the history of the Bundesliga. Germany played outstanding defense, only giving up four goals in seven games, though one came in a 1–0 loss to East Germany, an intensely emotional game. In the final, Germany defeated the Netherlands and the dazzling Johan Cruyff, 2–1, successfully man-marking Cruyff and shutting down the Dutch passing game.

In 1977, still at the top of his game, Beckenbauer signed a four-year, $2 million contract to play for the

New York Cosmos, alongside Pelé. He retired from international play at the same time.

"I had everything," Beckenbauer said of his decision. "I was the captain of Bayern Munich and of the German national team. Then the offer of the Cosmos came and I said, 'I don't know, I don't know.' . . . Pelé was my idol since '58 and I was a thirteen-year-old. It was a good chance to play with the best player of all time."

After becoming so famous and identifiable in Germany, he loved living in New York, where he was rarely recognized. In four seasons, the star-laden Cosmos won three championships.

"As a player he was marked out by intelligence rather than strength," Pelé said.

In 1980, Beckenbauer returned to Germany, where he played two seasons for Hamburg and helped his team win the Bundesliga title in 1982. Then he went back to New York to play for the Cosmos for one final season before hanging up his boots for good.

But Beckenbauer still had a full soccer life ahead of him. In 1984, he decided to use his leadership abilities in a new capacity and became the head coach of the West German national team. Just two years later, he guided West Germany to the final against Argentina. The Germans lost to Diego Maradona, but Beckenbauer was clearly a fit for the job.

Four years later, in Italy in 1990, Beckenbauer reached what he called his greatest achievement in soccer. He coached that last West German team before German reunification to a World Cup victory, winning a finals rematch over Argentina.

"It doesn't come any better than managing a side to victory," he said.

Beckenbauer managed the French club Marseille for a short time and then returned to Bayern Munich, managing the club for two separate short spells, during which time it won the Bundesliga title and the UEFA Cup. He served as club president for several years and served as chairman of the advisory board. Beckenbauer has been given credit for much of the success of Bayern Munich because of his smart management.

He headed up the organizing committee for the 2006 World Cup, which was held in Germany. It was one of the largest events to take place in unified Germany and brought immense pride to the Germans, in much the same way that "The Miracle of Bern" had when Beckenbauer was a small boy.

Throughout the history of post–World War II Germany, perhaps the most inspirational athlete in the country was Franz Beckenbauer.

STATISTICS:

Position: sweeper

Appearances for West German national team:
    103

Goals for West Germany: 14

Professional appearances (three clubs): 572

Goals for professional clubs: 83

XAVI

For almost a decade, Spain played some of the most beautiful and entertaining soccer the world had ever seen—the perfection of the "tiki-taka" system of possession football played by a "golden generation" of fabulous players.

Who was the most important player of that generation? Goalkeeper Iker Casillas, one of the best in the world? Perhaps the world's best defensive midfielder, Xabi Alonso? Goal scorers David Villa or Fernando Torres? Dazzling midfielder Andrés Iniesta?

All great players and great choices, but many consider midfielder Xavier Hernández Creus—better known simply as Xavi—to be the best Spanish player of the Golden Generation. And one of the best of all time.

Spain won two European Championships (2008 and 2012) and the 2010 World Cup with ball control and exquisite passing, a synchronous marriage of players and possession. And the player who executed the system to perfection was five-foot-seven Xavi, who earned the nickname "The Puppet Master" for his ability to dictate the pace of a game.

"That's what I do: look for spaces," he said of his game. "All day, I'm always looking."

His manager, Pep Guardiola, described his style as "I get the ball, I give the ball. I get the ball, I give the ball."

Such a style doesn't steal headlines or win individual awards, but it creates a dominant, winning system in which everyone succeeds.

"I don't win prizes," Xavi said. "I construct them. I get more enjoyment out of giving an assist than scoring a goal."

A native of Catalonia, Spain, born in a city outside Barcelona, Xavi had a role model in his father. Joaquim Hernández played for Sabadell, a nearby team. He mentored his son, who also loved to watch English football while he was growing up.

Xavi came up through Barcelona's youth system, beginning at age eleven. He made his senior team debut in 1998. He quickly became a key member of the team that won a title that year, and he was named La Liga Breakthrough Player of the Year the next year. He was a transitional player, the bridge between players like Guardiola, who played for Barcelona in the 1990s and later became Xavi's coach, and the Golden Generation.

But in the beginning of the 2000s, Barcelona struggled both financially and on the field. Xavi was there through it all, weathering some difficult years for Barcelona, until the team added some much-needed talent and reasserted its dominance.

In 2005, after a few years of mediocre performances, Barcelona won the La Liga title for the first time in six years, and Xavi was named the La Liga Player of the Year. He suffered an injury the next year but came back in time to be a substitute in Barcelona's win over Arsenal for the Champions League title.

Barcelona won five titles in the next seven years, and eight times in Xavi's career. He and his midfield partner, Andrés Iniesta, were the keys not only to Barcelona's success but to their country's success as well.

Spain had largely been considered an under-achiever in the world of soccer. The country's 1964

European Championship, won in its own country, was the lone major tournament title Spain had won before Xavi began his international career. As brilliant young talent came up, the nation was expected to do more.

Unfortunately, early on, expectations didn't turn into results.

In the 2000 Olympics, Xavi's team lost in penalty kicks in the gold medal match to Cameroon. In the 2002 World Cup, Spain was ousted in the quarterfinals on penalty kicks to host South Korea. In the 2004 European Championship, Spain didn't make it out of group play, and in the 2006 World Cup, Spain lost to France in the round of 16.

It was a frustrating pattern, but Xavi and his teammates broke through in a big way. In the 2008 European Championships, Spain won its first major title in forty-four years, beating Germany 1–0 in the final. Xavi was named the player of the tournament, with the technical committee determining that he "epitomizes the Spanish style of play."

"He is the best player in the history of Spanish football," Lionel Messi said.

Spain's run was just beginning. Unlike past

versions of the Spanish team, "La Roja" of 2008–2012 was a team that put aside the divisions that had too often split Spain—what dialect they spoke, whether they played for Barcelona or Real Madrid. Some of the differences were rooted deep in politics: Catalonia had a fierce independence movement and didn't consider itself part of Spain. But the Spanish soccer team was able to unite the country, and Xavi, a Catalonian, made a point of saying *"Viva España,"* a rally cry of national support that means "Long Live Spain."

The team's finest moment came in 2010 in South Africa, when Spain won the World Cup for the first time in its history. Xavi completed 91 percent of his passes, keeping the Spanish attack moving and organized.

"If football was a science, Xavi would have discovered the formula," said Jorge Valdano, the former coach of Real Madrid. "With a ball at his feet, no one else has ever communicated so intelligently with every player on the pitch."

In the European Championship in 2010, Spain again won the trophy, and Xavi again was instrumental in the team's success. Spain defeated Italy 4–0 in the final.

After Spain was ousted from the 2014 World Cup

in the group stage, Xavi retired from the team. He played one more season for Barcelona, making his final appearance as a substitute in the Champions League final, which Barcelona won. As captain of the team, Xavi lifted the trophy after the victory over Juventus. It was his fourth Champions League title.

Xavi went on to play for Al Sadd in Qatar. His three-year contract also included a role as an ambassador for the 2022 World Cup to be held in Qatar and an agreement to get his coaching license. Xavi expressed a desire to return to Barcelona and coach his old team in the future. But he was also critical of Barcelona, saying the team had "fallen asleep" in terms of its youth development and wasn't producing players out of its academy in the way it had in the past.

Xavi, of course, is an expert on the matter. He came out of Barcelona's academy system.

And went on to become one of the greatest players in history.

STATISTICS*:

Position: midfielder
Appearances for Spanish national team: 133
Goals for Spain: 13

Professional appearances (two clubs): 556
    (Barcelona 505, *Al Sadd 51)
Goals for professional clubs: 72 (Barcelona 58,
    Al Sadd 14)
*currently active player

JOHAN CRUYFF

The rise of the Netherlands as a world soccer power can pretty much be traced to one man: Johan Cruyff. Which is ironic, because he perfected the concept of the total team game.

Cruyff is not as famous to casual fans as Pelé or Maradona. But for a time he was considered the greatest player in the world. And he was the perfect example of the concept of Total Football, a philosophy in which any field player can take over the role of any other player and the team works seamlessly.

Although on paper, Cruyff played center forward, in the systems that he played in both professionally and for his country, he roamed the field, surprising and terrorizing opponents from every position. His teammates accommodated his movement in a fluid way that didn't weaken the team tactically.

"If he wanted, he could be the best player in any

position on the pitch," said former French player Eric Cantona.

Cruyff was born in Amsterdam in 1947 when the Netherlands was still recovering from World War II. He was raised in a working-class family, living just a few minutes from the stadium where Ajax—the most famous Dutch football team—played.

His father died of a heart attack when Cruyff was only twelve. After the family tragedy, his mother went to work for Ajax as a cleaning woman. Both events had an impact on Cruyff's determination to succeed as a soccer player. His father had loved the game and Cruyff wanted to honor his memory through his play. In addition, Cruyff's mother met her second husband through Ajax, who also worked there. He had a great deal of influence over the young boy.

By the time of his father's death, Cruyff was already playing on the Ajax youth team. He rose through the ranks of the club—even playing on the club's baseball side. Like many large sports clubs in Europe, the organization sponsored sports other than soccer. He made his senior team debut in 1964, at age seventeen. The next year, he established himself as a generational talent, scoring twenty-five goals in twenty-three games and leading Ajax's turnaround from a thirteenth-place finish to the league championship. Behind Cruyff, Ajax defended its title in 1967 and again in 1968.

The man directing this success was coach Rinus Michels. A former great Ajax player himself, Michels introduced the concept of Total Football and found the perfect artist to execute his vision in Cruyff. The flowing, visually pleasing style of football was embraced in Amsterdam at a time when the city was busy throwing off conventions and becoming a creative haven.

While at Ajax, Cruyff led the team to six league titles and three European Cups (now known as Champions League titles), and won the Ballon d'Or— as the world's best player—three times in four years: 1971, 1973, and 1974.

In 1973, he was transferred to Barcelona for approximately $2 million, a world-record fee at the time. He became a hero in the Catalonian part of Spain that supports Barcelona, leading the club to its first league title since 1960. He was reunited with his old coach Rinus Michels, who had moved on to coach Barcelona in 1971. Together they won the La Liga title. Cruyff stayed with Barcelona until 1978 and ended up making his home there for most of his life.

Cruyff was also a star on the Netherlands national team, making his debut in 1966. The Netherlands had not played in the World Cup since 1938, failing to qualify for five straight tournaments. The team finally qualified for the 1974 tournament, and after locking up the berth, Michels became the national head coach.

With Cruyff as the star, the Netherlands made a historic run, earning the nickname "Clockwork Orange" (a takeoff on both the title of a popular novel and the team's trademark color that alluded to the team's effective rotations). The Netherlands made it to the final, defeating Argentina and defending champion Brazil in the process, with Cruyff scoring three goals in those two matches, before losing 2–1 to host West Germany. Cruyff earned the Golden Ball as the top player in the tournament.

He helped the Netherlands qualify for the 1978 tournament but abruptly retired before the World Cup (where the Netherlands would again finish as the runner-up). At the time, it was believed that Cruyff— who was outspoken on social issues—did not want to play in Argentina, where a military dictatorship was in power. Many years later, he said his retirement was because of his fears of being away from his family, after an attempted kidnapping at their home in Barcelona.

During his career, Cruyff was considered a bit of a rebel. He spoke his mind and did things his way. For example, he refused to wear a uniform with the three stripes of Adidas, because he had a contract with Puma. So while his Dutch teammates had three stripes, Cruyff had just two on his jersey. He also chose jersey No. 14, breaking the tradition of wearing jerseys numbered from 1 to 11.

In his international career, he scored thirty-three goals in forty-eight games. He was famous for his philosophy about his sport, which he believed should be entertaining and beautiful to watch. He perfected a move called the Cruyff Turn, where he looked like he was about to pass the ball but instead dragged the ball behind his stationary leg with his other foot, turned 180 degrees, and sprinted away from the defender. He used it to perfection in the 1974 World Cup, and it is now a common tactic.

Cruyff briefly retired from professional soccer, but he had lost money in bad investments and returned to playing. He came to the United States and played in the NASL from 1979 to 1980, first in Los Angeles, where he won the NASL Player of the Year award in 1979, and then in Washington, D.C. He returned to play briefly in Spain, for Levante, and in the Netherlands, for both Ajax and its rival Feyenoord, before retiring for good.

After his playing days were over, Cruyff had a long and successful career as a coach, managing both Ajax and Barcelona. He played a crucial role in the development of many outstanding soccer stars, including Dennis Bergkamp and Pep Guardiola. In Barcelona, Cruyff's "Dream Team" won four La Liga titles and was a European power. He also helped establish Barcelona's "tiki-taka" soccer identity, which led to Spain's emergence as a global power. It was a legacy of the style he perfected as a player when he played for Michels, and it later became known as the "Barcelona style." The possession-oriented, short-passing game was the basis of Spain's successful run to the 2010 World Cup and the 2008 and 2012 European Championships, as so many of the national team players were raised in the system.

Cruyff also later served as technical director and advisor to both Barcelona and Ajax. But as time wore on, Cruyff, like his father, became ill at a fairly young age. A heavy smoker for much of his life, Cruyff had serious heart problems. He died of lung cancer in 2016.

His legacy and influence live on, however, in today's players and teams, even ones he never coached. Lionel Messi is a perfect example of the style of game that Cruyff promoted. Bayern Munich, influenced by Cruyff's pupil Pep Guardiola, also employs that style.

"Johan Cruyff painted the chapel," Guardiola once said. "And Barcelona coaches since merely restore or improve it."

Cruyff, both his style of play and his philosophy of soccer, changed the game forever. For the better.

"Quality without results is pointless," Cruyff once said. "Results without quality is boring."

And *boring* was not a word one would ever use to describe Cruyff.

STATISTICS:

Position: forward/attacking midfielder

Appearances for Netherlands national team: 48

Goals for Netherlands: 33

Professional appearances (seven clubs): 514

Goals for professional clubs: 290

ZINEDINE ZIDANE

A national hero. A public disgrace. A country uniter. A fan divider. A brilliant player. An equally brilliant coach.

Zinedine Zidane has fulfilled many roles in his soccer career. The French midfielder was one of the most talented players of his era. In later years, he became one of the standout coaches in professional soccer, guiding Real Madrid to consecutive Champions League titles.

Zidane was born in Marseille, France, in 1972. He was the son of Algerian immigrants who moved to France in the 1950s, prior to the Algerian War. The youngest of five children, Zidane grew up in a rough neighborhood. His father, Smail, worked in a warehouse and was an inspiration to his son.

"My father taught us that an immigrant must work twice as hard as anybody else, that he must never give up," Zidane once said.

Zidane learned to play soccer on the streets of his neighborhood, then played for local youth leagues. At age fourteen, he attended a French Football Federation training camp in Aix-en-Provence, in the south of France, where he was discovered by a scout for the club team AS Cannes.

Zidane went to Cannes for a short tryout and ended up staying for four years. He lived with the team director and his family. His coaches at Cannes noticed that the young player seemed to be driven by rage and was quick to retaliate against opponents or spectators who mocked his ethnicity or poor background. Keeping his emotions in check was one of his biggest challenges in Zidane's early years and would come back to haunt him on the world stage.

In 1992, at twenty, Zidane transferred to another French club, Bordeaux. He spent four years there before joining Juventus, based in Turin, Italy, in 1996. While he played in Italy, he became known as the best midfielder in the world. He led Juventus to two Serie A league titles and two Champions League finals. Zidane was a full-fledged superstar, but he became notable for not living the flashy life of other high-profile athletes. He was married and had four sons and was devoted to his family.

Zidane made his first appearance with the French national team in 1994, at age twenty-two. He was on the team that reached the semifinals of the European Championship in 1996, but he was not yet an established star.

In the 1998 World Cup, hosted in his home country, the world truly learned about "Zizou." France was not a heavy favorite, but it won all three of its games in group stage. In the last one, against Saudi Arabia, Zidane's fiery temper caught up with him as he was sent off for stomping on a player. He had to sit out France's 1–0 win over Paraguay in the round of 16. He was back for the team's quarterfinal victory over Italy and its semifinal win over Croatia.

Heading into the final against Brazil, France was a heavy underdog. Brazil was the defending World Cup champion, and its star Ronaldo was considered the greatest player in the world. But Ronaldo was mysteriously scratched from the lineup before the match, only to be reinserted minutes before game time. He played poorly. In contrast, France—behind the efforts of Zidane—dominated the game. Zidane scored two first-half goals, heading in corner kicks. The host country ended up winning the game 3–0, setting off delirious celebrations throughout Paris and the rest of France. A celebration on the famous Parisian avenue the Champs-Élysées attracted over a million people who saw Zidane's image screened on the famous monument the Arc de Triomphe, with the message "*Merci Zizou*," meaning "Thank you, Zizou."

France continued its strong run over the next couple of years, winning the European Championship in 2000. Zidane—who was named the FIFA World Player of the Year in both 1998 and 2000 and won the Ballon d'Or in 1998—was again the star of the team. Even when he wasn't scoring goals, he was a stellar playmaker, setting up goals with the perfect pass. He had become the best playmaker in the game.

"When Zidane stepped onto the pitch, the ten other guys just got suddenly better," said Swedish star Zlatan Ibrahimović "It is that simple. It was magic. He was more than good, he came from another planet. His teammates became like him when he was on the pitch."

In the 2002 World Cup, it became obvious how central he was to France's success when an injury kept him out of part of the tournament. Suffering from a thigh injury, Zidane missed France's first two games, rushed back for the third, and was ineffective. The defending World Cup champions were eliminated in group play without scoring a goal.

After France was eliminated from the 2004 European Championships in the quarterfinals, Zidane announced he was retiring from international soccer. But in 2005, he was persuaded to come out of retirement to help the struggling French team qualify for the 2006 World Cup. Though France had lost several players to retirement, Zidane helped lead the team back to the World Cup final. He earned the Golden Ball and was named Man of the Match in the semifinal.

For the first time since their victory in 1998, France—and Zidane—had returned to the World Cup final, this time against Italy. Zidane got off to a quick start. His penalty kick in the seventh minute of the match put France ahead early. Italy came back to tie, and eventually the match went into extra time.

Victory was within France's grasp. But in the 110th minute of extra time, Zidane lost his cool and headbutted Italy's Marco Materazzi in the chest. Zidane later said Materazzi had insulted his sister during play. As a result of the violent gesture, Zidane was sent off and was not available to his team in the penalty shootout. Italy won the final 5–3 on penalty kicks, and Zidane's infraction was considered the event that changed the game.

Despite the incident, Zidane remained immensely popular in France. Polls showed that more than 60 percent of the public forgave him. Some observed that it was refreshing to see such a superstar make a public mistake and have to deal with the aftermath.

Zidane later said that looking back on his career, the red cards he received were mostly a result of provocation.

"This isn't justification," he said. "This isn't an excuse. But my passion, temper, and blood made me react."

Zidane spent the final five years of his professional career with Real Madrid. He led Madrid to the Champions League title, with a goal over Bayer Leverkusen, in 2002. The team won La Liga in 2003 and Zidane was again the FIFA World Player of the Year. During his playing time with Real Madrid, he was part of a superstar-laden roster, playing alongside other stars like David Beckham, Luís Figo, and Brazilian star Ronaldo.

After his retirement from playing, Zidane retained

close ties to the club. He worked as a special advisor, then sporting director, then became the coach of the B team.

In early 2016, as Real Madrid struggled, the club fired its coach and hired Zidane midway through the season. Though many were skeptical of whether a superstar player would be a successful coach, he quickly grew into the role and got immediate results. Zidane led Real Madrid to back-to-back Champions League titles in 2016 and 2017, the first time any club had ever won consecutive titles in the history of the tournament.

Zidane, not far removed from his playing days, was able to relate to the talented players.

"Every piece of advice he gives you is like gold dust," midfielder Luka Modrić said. "It helps you improve on the pitch."

Zidane, who played for Real Madrid as an aging superstar, was credited, as a coach, for expertly handling his own superstar, Cristiano Ronaldo, persuading him to rest and save his energy for big moments. Under Zidane's guidance, Ronaldo had some of the best seasons of his achievement-filled career.

Not many players who are as brilliant as Zidane

was can find world-class success in a second career. But Zidane is, once again, one of the best in the world.

STATISTICS:

Position: attacking midfielder

Appearances for French national team: 108

Goals for France: 31

Professional appearances (four clubs): 506

Goals for professional clubs: 95

RONALDO

While there is no argument about the greatest Brazilian soccer player in history, you could spend hours debating who is the second best Brazilian player of all time, after Pelé.

Could it be Garrincha, who was overshadowed because he played alongside Pelé, but whose brilliant play helped Brazil win the 1962 World Cup after Pelé was injured? The spectacular midfielder Socrates? Romario, who led his team back to glory in the 1994 World Cup? Right back Cafu, who played in three World Cup finals? A new generation would argue that Neymar should be in the conversation.

Brazil's standard is set so high: World Cup finals and goals are the bar to clear. So for that reason, Ronaldo gets the nod here as the second most important player in Brazil's history and one of the most talented to ever play.

Nicknamed "The Phenomenon," he made four

World Cup teams, and for a time he held the record as the all-time World Cup scorer with fifteen goals.

Some believe that if he hadn't suffered so many injuries, Ronaldo would be considered the greatest player ever.

"Without hesitation, Ronaldo is the best player I ever played with," said Zinedine Zidane, who was Ronaldo's teammate on Real Madrid. "He had such an ease with the ball. He is number one. Every day I trained with him, I saw something different, something new, something beautiful."

Ronaldo, like almost all Brazilian stars, goes by just one name. He was born Ronaldo Luis Nazário de Lima in 1976 and grew up in poverty outside Rio de Janeiro. He dropped out of school at twelve and committed himself to playing soccer, first for Social Ramos Club in his neighborhood and then for São Cristóvão in the Carioca league.

He was spotted by former player Jairzinho, who recognized the teenager's enormous talent and recommended him to his former club, Cruzeiro. At age sixteen, Ronaldo debuted for Cruzeiro, one of Brazil's most successful teams. A few months after his debut, he scored five goals in a game and caught the attention of his country. He helped lead Cruzeiro to the 1993 Copa do Brasil, the club's first ever.

As his club career was taking off, Ronaldo was also in the Brazilian national team's youth system and was on the under-17 team that won a South American championship. In 1994, he made his debut with the national team in a friendly match against Argentina. He was included on the squad for the 1994 World Cup as a seventeen-year-old but did not play at all during Brazil's run to the championship.

At the 1996 Olympics, Ronaldo was on the team that won a bronze medal for Brazil. For a time, he went by the nickname "Ronaldinho" ("Little Ronaldo") because he played with other players named Ronaldo. Eventually, after the other, older Ronaldos retired, he became known as Ronaldo and in 1999 another player— Ronaldo de Assis—became known as Ronaldinho.

Ronaldo was embarking on what would be a complicated professional journey with many stops. In 1994, he went to PSV Eindhoven, because of the influence of his older teammate Romario, who played for the Netherlands club. He scored thirty goals in his first season, but his second season was cut short by a knee injury, a harbinger of what his future would hold.

His astounding scoring ability brought new suitors: both Inter Milan and Barcelona were interested in him, and Barcelona paid a then-world-record transfer fee of $19.5 million. Ronaldo didn't disappoint, scoring forty-seven goals in forty-nine games. He had such an incredible season—at just nineteen years old—that he was being called the best player in the world, better than Pelé, and became the youngest player to win the FIFA Player of the Year.

But long-term contract negotiations broke down with Barcelona, so Ronaldo was on the move again. In 1997, he moved on to Inter Milan, breaking the world record for a transfer fee again, at $27 million. During his years in Italy, he evolved into a more complete player, becoming a better defender and passer. He won the Player of the Year again, becoming the first player to win the award in consecutive years.

In 1998, Ronaldo, still only twenty-one, was at the height of his powers. The hype surrounding him before the World Cup in France was phenomenal: his gap-toothed smile, backed by the Nike swoosh, became the image of the tournament. Brazil, the defending champions, was the favorite and made it to the final, after beating the Netherlands on penalty kicks in the semifinal.

But the final, against host France, became one of the strangest and most mysterious events in World Cup history. About seventy minutes before the match, Ronaldo's name was not in the starting lineup. Half an hour later, Brazil's starting lineup was revised to include Ronaldo. But when he took the field, he looked nothing like the best player in the world, and France dominated, winning 3–0.

The world later learned that Ronaldo had suffered a convulsive fit in the afternoon, and then had fallen unconscious. When he awoke, he didn't know what had happened. While his team went to the Stade de France for the game, he went to the hospital. But then he came to the game, declared himself fit, and was put in the lineup. The odd circumstances launched a thousand conspiracy theories: that Brazil had thrown the game, that Nike had somehow conspired to create headlines, that Ronaldo had been poisoned.

The moment was the beginning of a difficult period for Ronaldo. The next year, playing for Inter Milan, Ronaldo suffered a devastating knee injury, rupturing a tendon in his right knee. Five months later, he tried to come back but injured the knee again. The injuries required two operations and interrupted his career, at a time when he was exceptional, for almost two years.

Because of Ronaldo's injuries, there were questions about Brazil heading into the 2002 World Cup, co-hosted by Japan and South Korea. Ronaldo had missed all of qualification. Despite that, he led Brazil to its fifth World Cup and was the top scorer with eight goals. Though he wasn't as explosive as he had been in the past, he was still a world-class player. And he won his third FIFA Player of the Year.

After the 2002 World Cup triumph that chased away some of the ghosts from 1998, Ronaldo moved on again, this time to Real Madrid. He was on a star-studded team, alongside Zidane and David Beckham. He played four seasons for Madrid, but at the end he struggled with weight gain and injury.

Those issues plagued him in the 2006 World Cup in Germany. However, Ronaldo could still score. With his third goal of the tournament, he broke the record for most goals scored in World Cup history (the mark was later broken by Miroslav Klose of Germany). The defending champions were beaten in the quarterfinals by France.

Ronaldo signed with AC Milan in January 2007. With the signing he became the first player to play for both of the fierce Italian rivals—AC and Inter Milan—as well as the Spanish rivals, Real Madrid and Barcelona. A year after the signing, Ronaldo suffered another serious knee injury, this time in his left knee. He was released at the end of the season and returned to Brazil to sign with Corinthians. He played for two seasons before retiring in 2011 at thirty-four, due to injuries and other physical problems.

He had influenced a generation. He had brought Brazilian soccer to the Netherlands, Italy, and Spain. And he also left a lot of people wondering what might have been if it hadn't been for devastating injuries.

"The best I have ever played against," said Italian goalkeeper Gianluigi Buffon. "If it wasn't for injury, I think he would be talked about on the same level as Pelé and Diego Maradona."

STATISTICS:

Position: forward
Appearances for Brazilian national team: 98
Goals for Brazil: 62
Professional appearances (seven clubs): 343
Goals for professional clubs: 247

PAOLO MALDINI

For decades Italian soccer was distinguished by its defense, a style called Catenaccio. The word is Italian for "door bolt," and the name implied a style that shut the opponents out of the goal.

For many years the steel in that bolt was Paolo Maldini, considered one of the top defenders to ever play the game. He played for the Italian national team for fourteen years, serving as its captain much of that time. And he played for AC Milan for an amazing twenty-four years, until he was forty-one years old.

When commenting on players he coached against famed Manchester United manager Sir Alex Ferguson said, "Without a doubt Paolo Maldini has been my favorite. He has a wonderful presence, competitive spirit, athleticism. And although not the world's greatest technically, he has influenced all the Milan teams during his wonderfully successful era."

Maldini was noted for his calm on the field, his work ethic, and his ability to read the game. Some players noted that when he marked them, they could never even get to the ball, let alone do any damage with it. Maldini was an intelligent, composed player who reportedly only received three red cards in his long, distinguished career.

"If I have to make a tackle," he once said, "then I have already made a mistake."

Maldini's destiny was laid out for him when he was born. His father, Cesare, played defense for Milan and for the Italian national team. His father served as captain of both teams and played in the 1962 World Cup. Cesare retired in 1967. A year later Paolo was born in Milan.

"I always dreamed about being as good as my dad," said Paolo, whose father transitioned into coaching when Paolo was just a toddler.

In fact, the son far surpassed the father.

He was a prodigy, who—after playing with Milan youth teams—made his debut with the senior team at age sixteen. By the next season, at seventeen, he was in the starting eleven. Though he originally played right back, he was switched to left back because of his ability with his left foot.

When Paolo was eighteen he was called up to the Italian under-21 team by a coach he knew quite well: his father.

"The situation was embarrassing because, for better or worse, there were always people willing to say that I was a favored son," Paolo once said.

That may be why he was so driven to prove himself. By nineteen, he was on Italy's senior national team and participated in the UEFA Cup, where Italy lost in the semifinals. By 1990 he was a regular on the team that hosted the World Cup. In the first of four World Cups he played in, he was part of a defense that didn't allow the opponent to score in its first four games. Finally, after 518 scoreless minutes, Italy relinquished a goal to Diego Maradona in the semifinal against Argentina. Italy ended up losing to Argentina on penalty kicks. The team finished third and Maldini was selected to the Team of the Tournament.

In the 1994 World Cup, Italy again rode its impressive defense, this time all the way to the final. After 120 minutes of scoreless soccer against Brazil, Italy was once again defeated on penalty kicks, 3–2. At the time, the most famous defender on the team was Franco Baresi. But Baresi was injured, other players were suspended because of penalties, and Maldini stepped up, playing both centerback and fullback. He was again named to the Team of the Tournament.

Italy's heartbreaking trend continued in 1998. Though the Azzurri (as they're known because of the sky blue or azure color of the team's jerseys) won its group, it lost in the quarterfinals to host and eventual champion France on penalty kicks. By the 1998 World Cup, Maldini was Italy's full-time captain.

France had Italy's number again in the 2000 European Championship, when Les Blues defeated Italy in extra time. At Maldini's final World Cup, in 2002, the Italians were eliminated by co-hosts South Korea, in the round of 16. The game was one of the most controversial in history: Italy's apparent winning goal was called offsides, attacking midfielder Francesco Totti was sent off, leaving Italy a man down, and the Italian coach accused the head official of fixing the game for South Korea!

Maldini, at age thirty-four, retired from international soccer after Italy was ousted. He was Italy's most capped player. Though he would never hoist a trophy, he played in twenty-three World Cup games and holds the record for most World Cup minutes played at 2,217.

If only he could've held on for another cycle, he would've captured that elusive championship—Italy won the 2006 World Cup.

But Maldini continued to play for AC Milan for several more years. He was the captain of Milan; his nickname "Il Capitano" came from wearing the captain's armband for so long for both country and club.

In his almost quarter century with Milan, Maldini had more success than he did with the Italian national team. His teams won five Champions League titles and seven Serie A titles.

In 2003, in the first Milan game in which he wore the captain's armband, Maldini's team beat Juventus in the Champions League final, Maldini's fourth title. It was the first all-Italian final, and it came exactly forty years to the day after his father had won the European Cup—what the Champions League was previously called—as Milan's captain. Maldini was named Man of the Match.

Maldini would captain Milan to a fifth title in 2007, becoming the oldest captain to hold the trophy, at age thirty-eight. Maldini announced that he would retire at the end of the 2009 season, at age forty-one.

His No. 3 jersey was retired by Milan. Over the

years he won many awards and honors, including being named Serie A Defender of the Year (2004), World Soccer Player of the Year (1994), and UEFA Defender of the Year (2007). He was selected to the Italian Football Hall of Fame, the AC Milan Hall of Fame, and the FIFA Order of Merit, and he was included on the World Soccer Greatest XI of all time list and the UEFA Euro All-time XI.

"Paolo Maldini is the best I've played against," said Brazilian great Ronaldo.

Ever the dynamic athlete, in 2017, at forty-nine, Maldini even tried his hand at professional tennis, playing doubles on the ATP Challengers Tour. He and his partner were quickly defeated (6–1, 6–1) in their debut.

"It's still sport but certainly not one I excel in," Maldini said.

For all his struggles on the tennis court, he excelled at soccer. And he's continuing his family tradition. Both his sons, Christian and Daniel, have been signed by Milan youth clubs. In 2016, Christian captained Milan's U-19 team in a friendly match. Christian played center or left back. Daniel, who was playing with Milan's U-16 team, is a striker.

When Maldini's jersey was retired, the club noted that it would not be worn again, unless one of his sons played on the senior team and wore it.

So there may be another No. 3 for Milan someday.

STATISTICS:

Position: left back, center back

Appearances for Italian national team: 126

Goals for Italy: 7

Appearances for AC Milan: 647

Goals for AC Milan: 29

GIANLUIGI BUFFON

Choosing the best goalkeeper of all time is a difficult task.

The Soviet Union's Lev Yashin was a legend in the early 1960s and is considered a player who redefined the art of goalkeeping with his athleticism and vocal command of the defense. Both Oliver Kahn and Manuel Neuer are legends in Germany. Spain's loyalty is to Iker Casillas. Danish fans will insist on Peter Schmeichel, and the English are certain Gordon Banks was the best ever.

But if one factors in longevity, leadership, skill, and winning for both club and country, then the best goalkeeper of all time is Italy's Gianluigi Buffon.

"Buffon was a role model to me," Neuer said.

For more than twenty years, Buffon was a constant in goal, for both Italy and his professional club, first Parma and then Juventus. He helped Italy win the World Cup in 2006. He helped Parma win the UEFA Cup in 1999. Eighteen years later, he captained Juventus into its second Champions League final in three years (Juventus lost both, to Barcelona and Real Madrid). The span of his career was astonishing.

"This is the beauty of life, the beauty of living," Buffon said. "Being able to meet guys who were not even born by the time you had a big part of your career behind you."

As a goalkeeper he was known for his quick reflexes and shot-stopping ability. He was always praised for his leadership, on and off the field; his vocal direction of the defense; and his mental strength, a key for goalkeepers.

Buffon was destined for an athletic career. His mother was a discus thrower and his father was a weightlifter, and later, both were physical education teachers. His sisters played volleyball for the national team, his uncle played basketball, and goalkeeping legend Lorenzo Buffon was a distant cousin.

He was born in Carrara, Italy, a town famous for the white marble quarried there, used in such works of art as Michelangelo's *David* statue. Buffon would make the town famous for his art in goal.

He started his youth soccer career as a midfielder but switched to goalkeeper at age eleven. When he was twelve, he became transfixed by the goalkeeping performance of Thomas N'Kono of Cameroon during the 1990 World Cup, which was held in Italy. When he joined Parma's youth system at thirteen, it was as a goalkeeper.

Buffon made his Serie A debut with Parma's senior team when he was seventeen. His clean sheet (shutout) in that start against Milan was a sign of things to come. He set a Serie A record for the most shutouts. By his second season, he had become the starting goalkeeper.

Early in his career, he earned the nickname "Superman," for stopping a penalty shot by Ronaldo, who played for Inter Milan and at the time was considered the most dangerous striker in the world. After the victory, Buffon celebrated by flashing the Superman shirt he wore under his Parma jersey. The name stuck and the next season seemed fully appropriate: Buffon helped Parma win the UEFA Cup, shutting out Marseille in the final.

In 2001 Buffon was transferred to Juventus for a fee that was a world record for a goalkeeper. During his long career at Juventus, he had enormous success but also faced scandal. In 2006 several players, including Buffon, were accused of illegally betting on Serie A soccer matches. Athletes are not allowed to bet on their own league's games. Buffon cooperated with the investigators, admitted to betting on sports, but denied betting on Italian soccer. He was cleared of all charges, but as a punishment, Juventus had their two most recent Serie A titles stripped and the team was relegated to Serie B.

Within a year Juventus was back in Serie A. Though Buffon suffered some injuries in the following seasons, he and his team regained form. After 2011, Juventus entered a new era of dominance. Juventus won six consecutive Serie A titles and made it back to the Champions League final twice, losing both in 2015 and 2017. In his sixteen-year career with Juventus (as of summer 2017), Buffon has been an invaluable member of the team.

Meanwhile, in the world of international soccer, Buffon was a regular on Italian youth teams from age fourteen on. In 1996, he represented Italy at the Olympics, which—on the men's side—is an under-23 tournament. He made his first appearance on the senior national team in 1997, when he was nineteen.

He helped the team qualify for the 1998 World Cup and was a member of the squad, originally as a third-string goalkeeper, but then he was promoted to backup due to an injury. However, he didn't play at all in the tournament, in which Italy lost in the quarterfinals on penalties to eventual champion France.

Buffon broke his hand before the 2000 European Championships and wasn't part of the successful run, in which Italy made it to the final. Francesco Toldo was the goalkeeper for that run and held on to the job during the qualifying round for the 2002 World Cup. But Buffon, clearly the goalkeeper of the future, regained his spot and played every minute of Italy's run in the 2002 World Cup and the 2004 European Championship. However, Italy's performance in both tournaments was disappointing to the Azzurri fans who expected championships.

Their wait was over in 2006. Italy had a dream run in the World Cup in Germany, and Buffon was excellent. He gave up just two goals: an own goal by a teammate and a penalty kick to Zinedine Zidane in the final against France. Overall, Buffon had five clean sheets and a 453-minute scoreless streak. Though neither Buffon nor his French counterpart Fabien Barthez saved a penalty in the finale of the championship game, Italy won when a French player missed. Buffon was named the goalkeeper of the tournament, elected to the Team of the Tournament, and finished second in the Ballon d'Or voting.

Buffon struggled with injury in the 2010 World Cup, which didn't help the defending champions, who were ousted without winning a game. Buffon became the acting captain of Italy, and in the 2012 European Championship he helped his side reach the final before being defeated by Spain. But in the 2014 World Cup, Italy was again eliminated in group stage and only made it to the quarterfinals of the 2016 European Championship.

Buffon continued to lead Italy into the 2018 World Cup cycle. In March 2017, in a World Cup qualifier against Albania, he earned his 1000th career appearance, with yet another clean sheet (his 426th for both club and country).

Buffon announced he would retire from international play after the World Cup in Russia. But in November of 2017, Italy fell to Sweden in a playoff, and was eliminated from a World Cup berth. The soccer world was shocked.

"I am not sorry for myself but all of Italian football," Buffon said, in tears after the elimination.

The loss meant the end of an amazing career that spanned generations and was an Italian constant, both for his club and his country.

A career that is one of the greatest in history.

STATISTICS*:

Position: goalkeeper

Appearances for Italian national team: 167

Clean sheets for Italy: 57

Professional appearances (two clubs): 894
*   (Parma 220, Juventus 674)*

Clean sheets for professional clubs: 426

*currently active player

TOP TEN BEST GOALS IN WORLD CUP HISTORY

10. **LANDON DONOVAN**, USA VS. ALGERIA, 2010, GROUP STAGE

After a disappointing performance in 2006 and two surprising draws in their opening matches of the 2010 World Cup, the Americans needed a victory against Ghana to stave off elimination. A draw would not be enough. One possible goal was disallowed due to a controversial offside call. The game was scoreless and the U.S. team appeared to be running out of time, with only one minute of injury time added. But in stoppage time, goalkeeper Tim Howard threw a long outlet pass to Donovan, who passed to Jozy Altidore, who passed to Clint Dempsey. Dempsey's shot was blocked, but Donovan, trailing Dempsey, hammered home the rebound! The win put the Americans through into the knockout round.

9. **ROBIN VAN PERSIE**, NETHERLANDS VS. SPAIN, 2014, GROUP STAGE

It wasn't hard to come up with a nickname for this goal: "The Flying Dutchman" was both obvious and perfect, considering Robin van Persie hailed from the Netherlands. The defending champions, meeting the team they had defeated four years earlier, Spain, had gone up 1–0 in the first game of their title defense in the 2014 World Cup. Then van Persie received a long ball from a teammate about 15 yards out from goal, launching himself toward the pass with his head, hitting it straight on, and looping it past goalkeeper Iker Casillas. Netherlands would destroy Spain 5–1 in the game, a sign of the losing team's early exit to come. The flying goal was one of the highlights of the entire tournament.

8. **ANDRÉS INIESTA**, SPAIN VS. NETHERLANDS, 2010, FINAL

Spain was the favorite to win the 2010 World Cup, but it had trouble scoring against the physical Dutch team. The foul-plagued game was scoreless deep into the second period of extra time. The Dutch were playing a man down after John Heitinga was sent off. Spanish midfielder Cesc Fabregas found a loose ball in the middle of the Dutch goal and passed it right to teammate Iniesta, who knocked it in over a charging defender and just past the reach of the goalkeeper to give Spain its first-ever World Cup.

7. **MARCO TARDELLI**, ITALY VS. WEST GERMANY, 1982, FINAL

The second goal in what would be a 3–1 win over Germany in the 1982 World Cup final was a beautiful counterattacking goal that was touched by seven players before Italian midfielder Tardelli had his moment of glory. The Italians passed the ball in front of Germany's net before finding Tardelli in the center about 20 yards out. He received the ball with his right foot, flicked it to his left, and hit a left-footed diagonal rocket that set off celebrations around Italy.

6. **GEOFF HURST**, ENGLAND VS. WEST GERMANY, 1966, FINAL

Hurst scored a hat trick, the only person ever to do so in a World Cup final until Carli Lloyd matched the achievement in 2015. Eleven minutes into the first extra time period, the game was tied 2–2 when Hurst gave the host team the lead, receiving a pass at the front of the goal and hammering it hard with his right foot. The ball hit the top netting and bounced down within a hair of the line. While Germany protested that it wasn't a goal—and would continue to do so for decades—it was ruled a goal (a decision upheld later when goal line technology reviewed it). Hurst added his historic third goal deep into extra time, and it was the controversial game-winner that will always be remembered.

5. **ZINEDINE ZIDANE**, FRANCE VS. BRAZIL, 1998, FINAL

Most observers say that of France's three shocking goals against Brazil in the 1998

World Cup final, the prettiest was the last by Emmanuel Petit. But Zidane set the tone in the 27th minute, leaping high in the air, legs splayed, to head in a corner kick and give France a surprising 1–0 lead. He would score a replica less than twenty minutes later.

4. JOHAN CRUYFF, NETHERLANDS VS. BRAZIL, 1974, GROUP STAGE

Cruyff led the Netherlands into the final and became famous for the Cruyff Turn. But this goal against Brazil that put the Dutch into the finals was a beauty. After a game of being viciously fouled and relentlessly double-teamed, Cruyff had already had an assist on his team's first goal. In the 65th minute he crashed the goal and made a leaping left-footed shot into the net to seal the win.

3. CARLOS ALBERTO, BRAZIL VS. ITALY, 1970, FINAL

This was the last World Cup championship for Pelé and the last for twenty-four years for Brazil. Though the game was already decided when this goal was scored in the 86th minute, it was one for the ages. Brazil brought the ball up; Pelé received a pass in the middle and waited for the right moment to find Carlos Alberto flying down the right side. A prime example of *jogo bonito*, the Brazilian term for the "beautiful game."

2. PELÉ, BRAZIL VS. SWEDEN, 1958, FINAL

This goal was the moment the star was born. The seventeen-year-old trapped the ball with his chest, flicked it high over a defender, and buried it in the back of the net. The goal, his first of two in the game, proved to be the winner and led Brazil to its first-ever world championship.

1. DIEGO MARADONA, ARGENTINA VS. ENGLAND, 1986, QUARTERFINALS

There's a reason it's still called the Goal of the Century more than twenty years after it happened and well into a new century. Argentina's superstar had already broken

England with the Hand of God goal, and then the Lions watched helplessly as Maradona danced past five defenders and dribbled around goalkeeper Peter Shilton before hitting the back of the net. Argentina won the World Cup, but the quarterfinal goal remains the tournament's highlight.

▶ ▶ ▶ *HALFTIME*

LEAGUES AROUND THE WORLD

Soccer is a sport of many allegiances. You may be American but root for Spain because your favorite player on a team in the English Premier League is Spanish. And get ready to change your allegiance at a moment's notice, because that player could be transferred to a German club soon.

While the World Cup is soccer's premier event every four years, there is fantastic club competition all year long. In the twenty-first century, with expanded TV rights and live streaming, the top clubs in the world have become accessible to soccer fans everywhere.

Now allegiances and enthusiasm cross cultures and borders, and the best players in the world are often household names, far from home.

In addition to league competitions, the top European clubs from different leagues compete each year in the Union of European Football Associations (UEFA) championship (previously called the European Cup). That competition brings together most of the biggest stars on the globe, in games that take place throughout the season, culminating with the championship games in May.

Many professional leagues adopt the relegation and promotion system, where teams have to meet a certain standard to stay in the top division. If they do not, they are "relegated" to second division. If they achieve, they are "promoted" to a higher level. However, the system is not used in U.S. sports leagues, including Major League Soccer.

In an era where soccer leagues continue to expand far and wide, it can be hard to keep track of it all. Don't worry—I've got you covered. Here's a look at some of the top professional leagues around the world.

ENGLISH PREMIER LEAGUE (EPL)

England has the oldest professional league. And though England has had plenty of global competition, the EPL is still considered the gold standard of professional soccer.

The roots of the league are in the Football League, which was founded in 1888 and consisted of twelve teams in one division. When additional teams were added four years later, it was split into two divisions. That system existed for 100 years, until 1992, when the top teams left to become the Premier League. The impetus was a huge TV deal: the EPL is now the most-watched league in the world.

The top twenty teams make up the Premier League. At the end of the season, the three lowest-placed teams are relegated to the lower-division Football League Championship, and the two highest-ranked Football League Championship teams are automatically elevated to the Premier League, while there is a playoff for the third promotional spot.

Despite the plethora of teams, only a handful have dominated competition. Four teams have won all but two of the EPL championships: Manchester United, Chelsea, Arsenal, and—twice—Manchester City. Blackburn won one championship in 1995. The biggest surprise of all was when Leicester City won the title in 2016.

Manchester United is considered the most popular club in the world. In its history, some of the most recognized players on the planet have worn the red jersey, including David Beckham, Cristiano Ronaldo, George Best, Wayne Rooney, Bobby Charlton, and Ryan Giggs.

Succeeding in the EPL is an honor, which is why

American players like Tim Howard and Clint Dempsey are so respected for their ability to have played well in the EPL.

LA LIGA

The Spanish first-division league has emerged as the top league in European soccer, winning more UEFA championships so far in the twenty-first century than any other league.

The league gained popularity and global status thanks to the rivalry and star power of its top two teams, Real Madrid and FC Barcelona. The rivals combined for nine UEFA championships between 2000 and 2017. Real Madrid has won the UEFA title a record twelve times!

The fact that the two men considered the best players in the world—Lionel Messi and Cristiano Ronaldo—plied their trade in La Liga and competed against each other for years only added to the league's glamour.

The league was started in 1927 with ten teams. It now has twenty teams and a system of promotion and relegation, with the lowest-rated teams dropped to the Segunda Division at the end of each season.

La Liga has a more political history than many leagues. The Spanish Civil War started shortly after the league formed, and the divisions continue to this day. Barcelona's crest became a symbol for an independent Catalonia, the region where the team is based, which has vied to become its own separate country for decades. Real Madrid was the team associated with dictator Francisco Franco, and even half a century after his death, fans remember those oppressive ties. Athletic Bilbao is a symbol of the Basque independence movement, in another region that has toyed with the idea of forming its own country.

While the Premier League is the richest soccer league in the world, La Liga is the only league to boast two of the top three teams in terms of revenue: Real Madrid and Barcelona. The Spanish team that won the World Cup in 2010 was made up almost exclusively of players from those two clubs.

BUNDESLIGA

German soccer lagged behind other countries in terms of establishing a strong professional league, in part because of its history in World War II and subsequent separation into two countries.

Prior to the formation of the Bundesliga in 1963, soccer was played in Germany only at a semiprofessional level, which caused some of the best German players to leave the country to play abroad. Without a strong national league to nurture its homegrown players, the German national team began to falter, increasing the impetus to form a world-class professional league.

The Bundesliga was launched with sixteen teams. After the reunification of Germany in 1990, the league expanded and currently has eighteen teams. It uses a system of relegation and promotion with teams sent to the second division. The league is proud to boast of some of the lowest ticket prices in Europe and overall highest attendance.

The most successful club is Bayern Munich, which has won the Bundesliga title twelve times and the European Championship five times. Bayern Munich, which was formed in 1900, existed before the creation of the Bundesliga as a member of various semiprofessional leagues and flourished early on. But its progress was hurt by the rise of the Nazi party, when Bayern

Munich's Jewish president and coach had to flee the country.

But the club's fortunes changed again in the early 1960s, when the team joined the Bundesliga and added player Franz Beckenbauer to its senior roster. Beckenbauer led the team to three European Cups.

In more recent years, Bayern Munich has been home to several of the top German players, including many on the 2014 World Cup winning roster, such as goalkeeper Manuel Neuer and midfielders Thomas Müller and Bastian Schweinsteiger.

SERIE A

The Italian first division is home to some of the most successful clubs in soccer history, and in the twentieth century it was widely considered the top league in the world. Though it may have been surpassed by some other leagues in the twenty-first century, notably La Liga, it is still home to exciting soccer and top players.

The league dates back to 1898, though at the time, teams were divided by region. In 1929 the league became centralized into Serie A, with eighteen teams.

There are currently twenty teams. The league, which has a system of relegation and promotion, was ranked fourth in UEFA, behind the three leagues mentioned earlier.

The only club to compete in Serie A in every season since its founding is Inter Milan. Juventus, based in the city of Turin, is the most successful team, dominating in the 1930s, 1970s, and 1980s and for most of the twenty-first century.

Some of the most famous players in the world have played in Serie A, like Kaká and Ronaldo from Brazil and France's Zinedine Zidane. However, most of the Serie A record holders are Italian. Paolo Maldini holds the record for most appearances, 647, all with AC Milan. Gianluigi Buffon is second, playing for both Parma and Juventus. The top goal scorers for the league are Silvio Piola and Francesco Totti, who both led Italy to World Cups in different eras.

MAJOR LEAGUE SOCCER (MLS)

Major League Soccer is not one of the top soccer leagues in the world. Not yet. But its promoters hope it will be soon.

After all, MLS is one of the younger leagues in the world. The United States didn't have a successful professional soccer league when the 1994 World Cup was awarded to the country in 1988. The North American Soccer League had briefly flourished in the 1970s thanks to the arrival of several high-profile players, most notably Pelé.

But that phenomenon had come and gone. When FIFA awarded its prize tournament to the United States, one of the conditions was that the country would create a viable professional league. And in 1996, the league was born.

The league started with ten clubs, all with a franchise player from the men's national team. Though some of the team names have changed or been "rebranded," nine of those original ten remain. By 2017 the league had expanded to twenty-two teams and was planning further expansion.

Though the league struggled in its early years, playing in enormous NFL stadiums for the most part, it began to find its footing in the early twenty-first century. It was helped by young American talent like Landon Donovan and others who became stars. (More on them in the next chapter.) The league also invested in smaller, soccer-specific stadiums that gave fans an intimate experience.

The league adopted a "designated player" rule in 2007 and some global stars joined the league, most notably David Beckham, who came to the Los Angeles Galaxy. Though the star power created attention and a spotlight, it didn't do much to improve the quality of play. Many wondered if the league would catch on, especially since American soccer fans could watch the best international competition in the world on television. The league also faced criticism because it played a backward schedule to the rest of the world, starting in the spring and ending in the fall. That decision was made so that the sport would take place during the summer months, which are a slower time on the American sports calendar.

But as the years went on, the level of play improved. The teams gained devoted followings. MLS teams began academies, emulating European clubs, in order to develop homegrown prospects who could help not only their clubs but the national team and also be sold to foreign clubs. The league increased in financial value, and expansion plans were greeted with enthusiasm.

MLS was almost a century behind other nations' professional soccer leagues. It has come a long way fast.

SOME OF THE OTHER TOP LEAGUES IN THE WORLD

FRENCH LIGUE 1:
The top French league has twenty teams, including Paris Saint-Germain, Lyon, Saint-Étienne, and Marseille.

PRIMEIRA LIGA:
Portugal's top league is made up of eighteen teams, including Benfica, Porto, and Sporting CP.

EREDIVISIE:
The top Dutch professional league has eighteen teams, including Ajax, PSV Eindhoven, and Feyenoord.

LIGA MX:
Mexico's top league has eighteen teams, including Club América, Guadalajara, Atlas, Pachuca, and Toluca.

ARGENTINE PRIMERA:

Argentina's professional league has twenty-eight teams, including River Plate, Boca Juniors, Racing, and Newell's Old Boys.

BRASILEIRO SERIE A:

Brazil's top league is home to twenty teams, including such famous clubs as Corinthians, Santos, Fluminense, and Flamengo.

MOST WORLD CUP
CHAMPIONSHIPS BY COUNTRY

4. **(TIE) FRANCE**: 1 (1998); ENGLAND: 1 (1966); SPAIN: 1 (2010)

3. **(TIE) ARGENTINA**: 2 (1978, 1986); URUGUAY: 2 (1930, 1950)

2. **(TIE) GERMANY**: 4 (1954, 1974, 1990, 2014); ITALY: 4 (1934, 1938, 1982, 2006)

1. **BRAZIL**: 5 (1958, 1962, 1970, 1994, 2002)

► ► ► **SECOND HALF**

THE AMERICAN STARTING 11

LANDON DONOVAN

The best male American soccer player was the same person in 2002 as it was in 2006 as it was in 2010. And until someone makes a strong claim to his throne soon, the king of American soccer continues to be Landon Donovan.

He is America's most important player.

In the first decade of the twenty-first century, Donovan evolved from teenage prodigy to American icon. His progress paralleled the American public's growing interest in the world's game.

Even years after his retirement, the United States was still searching for someone who could surpass him in terms of what he meant to the program and to the fortunes of his sport in America.

"He's the greatest player ever to pull on a U.S. shirt," said goalkeeper Tim Howard. "Anyone who argues with that, I think they're missing the whole point."

Donovan was born in Ontario, California, an inland suburb of Los Angeles. He was a twin—his sister, Tristan, came into the world first. His father, Tim, was estranged from the family for much of Donovan's childhood, and his mother, Donna, raised the twins and their older brother, Josh, mostly on her own.

Donovan started playing soccer with his older brother when he was about six. He was a natural. In his first organized game, he scored seven goals. He rose through the ranks of youth soccer and was chosen to play on the select club teams. Though money was tight, he often received scholarships from the clubs, which allowed him to continue to participate.

He was a star in high school and was invited to play in the U.S. Olympic Development Program. He played for the U.S. under-17 program, and the sixteen-year-old's talent caught the eye of German club Bayer Leverkusen, which scouted him playing at a youth tournament in Europe. When he was just seventeen, Donovan signed a six-year contract with the German club.

"In twenty-one years of working with young players, I have rarely seen such strong potential," said Michael Reschke, the director who signed Donovan.

Donovan's trademark was speed, vision, and tactical skill. He could play forward but was often at his most lethal on the wing.

"The problem with Landon is that he's your best player at so many positions that you never know where to put him," his longtime coach Bruce Arena once said.

Teenaged Donovan headed to Germany and though he played well, he wasn't happy. He had been a star at home, and suddenly every practice was an intense competition. As an American—and a very young one—he got little respect.

"If you are not in a situation that is good for you, it can be absolutely miserable," he said.

After two years of going back and forth between Germany and the States to play on national teams, Donovan requested and received a loan to return home and play for the San Jose Earthquakes of Major League Soccer (MLS). Just nineteen, he was an immediate success, leading the Earthquakes to an MLS championship. He played in twenty-two games, had seven goals and ten assists, was an All-Star, and was the MVP of the all-star game. He was starting to cause a stir in American soccer circles.

By that time, he had made his debut with the U.S.

senior national team, scoring a goal in his first match against Mexico, an opponent against whom he would thrive throughout his career. That debut came just a few weeks after he had played with the men's U-23 team at the Sydney Olympics. Under the guidance of new coach Bruce Arena, the senior team left behind the embarrassment of the 1998 World Cup, in which it failed to win a match, and was remade with key veterans and exciting, young players such as Donovan and DaMarcus Beasley.

Donovan's legend became firmly set in the 2002 World Cup. Little was expected of the Americans, but that changed when the team shocked Portugal in its opener. With the Americans up 1–0 in the 29th minute of the match, Donovan's cross toward the goal was deflected in by the Portuguese goalkeeper, giving the Americans a 2–0 lead. Donovan raised his hands in amazement—even he had not expected the ball to go in. The U.S. team won the match, 3–2.

As the group stage continued, the Americans went on to tie host South Korea before losing to Poland. But their efforts in the group stage allowed them to advance to the knockout round, where they faced rival Mexico.

In that game, Donovan scored in the 65th minute,

heading in a perfect cross from teammate Eddie Lewis, to give the Americans a 2–0 lead. With that victory, the U.S. team advanced to the quarterfinals for the first time in the modern era. The magical run ended in the quarterfinals in a narrow 1–0 loss to Germany.

Donovan returned to the United States to a hero's welcome and immediately became the new face of Major League Soccer. The following year, he led the Earthquakes to a second title.

America had finally found its male soccer star.

But as quickly as he'd arrived, in 2004, America— or at least MLS—briefly lost Donovan when he had to return to Bayer Leverkusen. Again, he was unhappy. He played in seven games but made just two starts and played poorly. His reputation as a player who could only perform when he was content and comfortable began to be etched in stone.

Donovan again requested a return to MLS, though he could not return to the Earthquakes since they had previously traded away his rights. In a bit of games-manship, to get the biggest star into the Los Angeles market, the Los Angeles Galaxy acquired his rights. Donovan was happy once again. He enjoyed living back in Southern California, near the beach. He signed a multiyear contract with the Galaxy, became the face of MLS, and won his third league title in 2005.

Thanks to his high profile, there were equally high expectations for the American team heading into the 2006 World Cup in Germany. But the team was eliminated in group play without winning any of its three games. Donovan, then in his prime at twenty-four, didn't provide any goals or assists, leading to criticism at home and jeers in Germany.

Donovan continued to play for the Galaxy, during a period when English superstar David Beckham was brought in, creating an awkward partnership during which Donovan often felt like the runner-up in a two-man contest.

As he got older, he became interested in once again playing in Europe. In late 2008, he went to Bayern Munich on a loan for several weeks. In 2010, he played for Everton on loan; though Everton was interested in retaining him, the Galaxy refused.

On the national team side, Donovan surpassed Eric Wynalda as the team's all-time leading scorer in 2008. He scored the free kick that gave the United States a win over Honduras and a berth in the 2010 World Cup in South Africa.

In South Africa, Donovan silenced any critics, coming up huge in the world spotlight and playing every minute of every game. He scored in the second match against Slovenia to help the team climb out of a 0–2 hole and salvage a tie. And in one of the most dramatic goals ever scored, Donovan's deep into-injury-time goal gave the United States a 1–0 win over Algeria and a berth in the knockout round.

With the seconds ticking down against Algeria, goalkeeper Tim Howard sent the ball as far downfield as he could, where Donovan—at a full sprint down the right flank—picked it up on a quick touch and headed toward goal. He looked for his teammate Jozy Altidore, who crossed to Clint Dempsey, who attempted a shot, but the ball deflected off the goalkeeper, and—still at full sprint—Donovan found the rebound in front of the net and buried it. Donovan slid belly first across the field in celebration, and in homes across the United States, the joy and excitement were equally wild.

In large part thanks to Donovan's impact, in the years since he had joined the national team, the American public's knowledge and appetite for the sport had grown in leaps.

Though the U.S. team lost to Ghana in the round

of 16, Donovan scored on a penalty kick, bringing his World Cup total to five goals. At the time, it was the most by any player in CONCACAF (the Confederation of North, Central American and Caribbean Association Football) history.

After the high of the World Cup ended, Donovan returned to Los Angeles. He went on to win three more MLS Cups with the Galaxy, under his former national team coach Bruce Arena. He again went on loan to Everton in late 2011 but didn't stay.

More than once, Donovan cited his desire to take a break from soccer, due to physical and emotional exhaustion. He took a sabbatical in 2013 and missed three World Cup qualifiers, causing a rift with new national team coach Jürgen Klinsmann, who subsequently left Donovan off the roster. The relationship between the two men was tense. But Donovan returned later that year to help the Americans win the Gold Cup and to qualify for the 2014 World Cup with a win over Mexico. Donovan had an assist and a goal in that qualifier.

When the United States opened training camp the next May, Donovan was in the pool, a veteran presence at thirty-two. But Klinsmann shockingly left Donovan off the World Cup squad in a controversial and heavily criticized decision. Though Donovan was older, and his mood was at times in question, he was the best player the U.S. team had ever produced and a savvy veteran presence that the Americans could have used in Brazil. At the 2014 World Cup, the U.S. team was, once again, eliminated in the round of 16. Whether or not Donovan could have made a difference, we will never know.

Donovan officially retired from the national team in October 2014, with a farewell game. He retired from the Galaxy two months later after winning his sixth MLS Cup, though he came briefly out of retirement in 2016. He retired as the all-time goal scorer in both MLS and U.S. national team history, though Clint Dempsey tied his national team record of fifty-seven goals in 2017.

After his playing career, Donovan went on to a broadcasting career with Fox Sports. He has been active in trying to get an MLS franchise in San Diego.

He was the first American field player who was truly considered world-class, a man who put American soccer on the map as a teenager and continued his brilliant career into adulthood.

He saw the bigger picture for his sport.

"Most of us are in this more than just for playing soccer," he said. "We're in it for a bigger goal—to move it along for the next generation."

Donovan helped achieve that goal. But until further notice, no one from the next generation has surpassed him. Not yet.

STATISTICS:

Position: midfielder/forward

Appearances for U.S. national team: 157

Goals for the United States: 57

Professional appearances: 398

Goals for professional clubs: 156

TIM HOWARD

For a generation of American soccer fans, seeing Tim Howard in goal was like having a security blanket. His constant, dependable presence made you feel safe and sound.

Howard, who started playing for the national team in 2002, was still chugging along at thirty-eight years old when the United States competed in the 2018 World Cup qualifiers. Sadly, he was in goal when the United States lost to Trinidad and Tobago in the final qualifier, meaning Howard would not make a fourth World Cup. During the many years of his career, both playing for his country and in the English Premier League, he established himself as one of the best goalkeepers of his era.

During the Howard era, American fans took to chanting "I Believe That We Will Win." And a huge part of that belief stemmed from the dominance of Team USA's goalkeeper.

"He's somebody who gives the group so much," said longtime teammate Michael Bradley. "You look back there and he's somebody who exudes confidence. He always finds a way to lift the group."

Howard grew up in New Jersey, in an apartment with his single mom and older brother. His mother's parents, Hungarian immigrants who escaped communist rule in 1956, lived nearby and shared stories with their grandsons about how they came to America with nothing and worked hard to build a good life in a new nation. Those stories inspired Howard.

Howard played many sports growing up, but he was drawn to soccer because of its fluidity and pace. Since he was tall and fearless, the coaches put him in goal. At first, he wasn't thrilled with playing the position, but he was very good.

When Howard was about ten, he started to develop symptoms: physical tics, facial jerks, throat-clearing, and obsessive touching of objects. Soon he received a diagnosis of Tourette syndrome (TS), an obsessive-compulsive disorder (OCD). He was very self-conscious about his condition, which was particularly difficult at an age when kids often feel insecure for other reasons.

Howard struggled in school but found an outlet in soccer, where he was able to succeed and focus absolutely on the task at hand: stopping the ball. In some ways, his condition, while a challenge in his day-to-day life, offered him "enhanced perception" on the field, as he stated in his memoir, *The Keeper*.

"I could see things somehow, things that other people didn't seem able to," Howard wrote. "I could see, for example when a game was about to shift, could sense the attacking patterns before they happened. I knew exactly when the winger was about to cross the ball and whose head it would land on. I could see the flicker of a striker's eyes before he pivoted."

Around the same time that he learned he had TS, he connected with a local goalkeeping coach, Tim Mulqueen—nicknamed "Coach Mulch"—that Howard credited with teaching him not only about goalkeeping but also about leadership.

Howard played positions in the field for his school soccer team and also played basketball. But as he moved up the ranks of club soccer teams, he was always a goalkeeper, and he eventually earned a spot in the Olympic Development Program, which led to a path to the national team programs, such as the under-15 team.

When Howard was fifteen, the 1994 World Cup was held in the United States. It helped make Howard's passion for soccer tangible as he saw the stars in action and analyzed their teams. His youth team went to a World Cup game between the United States and Colombia in California, and Howard watched starting American goalkeeper Tony Meola play and fantasized about being on the field.

It was a preview of days to come: Howard and some of his teammates on the youth national teams, like Carlos Bocanegra, would indeed become the future stars of the American team.

Before Howard graduated from high school, he was offered the chance to play professionally with a team called the New Jersey Imperials, a kind of minor-league team connected to the New York/New Jersey MetroStars, one of the franchises in the brand-new Major League Soccer. Coach Mulqueen had been hired as the MetroStars' goalkeeping coach, and he brought Howard into the system. Howard opted to turn pro rather than continue on with school by heading to college.

"This was a total leap of faith," he wrote in his memoir.

His efforts paid off. Within a year, he made it to the MetroStars as backup for Meola, the goalkeeper he had watched in the 1994 World Cup. He made his first start in August 1998, in which he made five saves in a 4–1 victory. By 2001, Howard was the starting goalkeeper for the MetroStars. He had also represented the United States at the 1999 FIFA World Youth Championship and the 1999 Pan-American games and was a backup at the 2000 Olympics in Sydney.

Howard also came out publicly about his TS and received the MLS award for Humanitarian of the Year, as well as Goalkeeper of the Year.

Early on, many people misunderstood Howard's disease, which resulted in a lot of embarrassment and ridicule for him. Fans didn't understand how he could communicate with his teammates. To the contrary, Howard established himself as a vocal leader, ordering his defense into position and commanding the organization of his teams. It wasn't as easy to change the public's perception of his TS, but over time, people learned that his talent spoke for itself, and he disproved the false, superstitious beliefs about his condition.

Howard had always dreamed of playing in Europe, ever since he was young. One day his phone rang with a feeler from Manchester United. Few Americans had ever had the chance to play with high-profile clubs, let alone the most famous in the world. Man U paid a $4 million transfer fee to sign Howard in the middle of the 2003 season, where he replaced famed French goalkeeper Fabien Barthez. It took a while to get a work permit, but eventually Howard made it to Manchester.

In the international spotlight, Howard played well and had to get used to being famous, as people would often approach him at restaurants or follow him around the grocery store. However, he made a critical mistake in March 2004 that led to a defeat in the Champions League. The error appeared to ruin manager Alex Ferguson's confidence in him and affected Howard's ability, as he continued to make more mistakes and was soon replaced in goal by Roy Carroll. For a season, they played musical chairs in goal. Eventually the team signed another keeper, Edwin van der Sar, who became the starter with Howard as the backup.

Howard tried to learn all he could from the more experienced goalkeeper. After one season as a backup in Manchester, he joined Everton on loan. Howard immediately felt comfortable in the Liverpool club and signed a permanent deal in 2007. He thrived over the next few years, breaking the club record for most clean sheets in a season in 2008–2009. He had a moment of retribution in 2009 in an FA Cup semifinal when he saved two penalties against Manchester United, eliminating his former team and sending Everton into the final, where it lost to Chelsea.

By that time, Howard had firmly established himself as a regular on the U.S. national team. Though he was a backup to Kasey Keller in the 2006 World Cup, by the 2009 Confederations Cup, he was the American starter. In that tournament, the Americans—after losing to Italy and Brazil—beat the No. 1 team in the world, Spain. Howard was instrumental in that victory, shutting out Spain.

Howard was the starting keeper in the 2010 World Cup in South Africa. The Americans had a difficult opening match against England. Howard was injured early in the match but kept playing. The game ended in a 1–1 draw, and Howard earned Man of the Match honors for his efforts. The next match, against Slovenia, ended in a 2–2 tie. In the final game of group play, against Algeria in extra time, Howard threw a long pass downfield, where Landon Donovan jumped on it, brought it downfield, and eventually buried a rebound in the net. The goal advanced the team to the round of 16, where the Americans lost 2–1 to Ghana.

Over the next few years, Howard continued to play for the United States. In 2011, the team made the transition from coach Bob Bradley to Jürgen Klinsmann. Klinsmann made a lot of changes to the team—including leaving Howard's friend Landon Donovan off the team—but he kept Howard in goal and even hired his Everton goalkeeping coach Chris Woods.

For the 2014 World Cup, the United States was drawn into the "Group of Death" against Ghana, Portugal, and Germany, and their tournament stint would include nine thousand miles of travel throughout Brazil. The Americans beat Ghana and tied Portugal 2–2 and lost to the eventual champions, Germany, 1–0. But they advanced to the second round, where they faced one of the favorites, Belgium.

In that game, Howard had his finest moment, making save after save after save as the talented Belgian players hammered him with shots. The game went into extra time scoreless, but in the first period Belgium scored two goals. In the second fifteen minutes of extra time, American Julian Green, a teenage substitute, scored in his first World Cup moment. But the Americans couldn't get the equalizer and lost.

In the game, Howard set a World Cup record with fifteen saves in a single game. The game spawned thousands of memes of "Things Tim Howard Could Save," including the *Titanic*, a swimmer from the shark in *Jaws*, and Ned Stark in *Game of Thrones*.

Over the following years, Howard became the face of the U.S. national team. But late in his career, he started to battle injuries, including two broken vertebrae. A knee injury slowed him in Everton, and he returned to Major League Soccer to play with Colorado. After his last game with Everton, he made an emotional speech.

"I will remain an Evertonian for life," he said. "This will always be my team, my club."

At the end of 2016, Howard suffered a groin injury while he was with Colorado Rapids. But when the Americans returned to the field in 2017 to attempt to qualify for the 2018 World Cup, Howard was back in goal.

"I have no reason to believe that Tim can't keep going," coach Bruce Arena said.

To the contrary. When Howard was in goal, it made Americans believe they could win.

STATISTICS*:

Position: goalkeeper

Appearances for U.S. national team: 121

Shutouts for the United States: 35

Professional appearances (four clubs): 625

*currently active player

JOE GAETJENS

The most startling goal in American soccer history wasn't scored by an American. But Joe Gaetjens was wearing the U.S. Soccer uniform when he scored the lone goal in the 1950 World Cup to beat England 1–0.

So he makes the American starting eleven.

Gaetjens's story is one of quirks and mystery, the kind that make soccer so fascinating. A Haitian, who could have been a German, instead played for the United States and knocked off the world favorites, England, became famous, and was later murdered in his homeland.

Gaetjens's amazing moment happened in 1950, in the World Cup in Brazil. It was the fourth World Cup ever held, and the first since 1938, with the tournament suspended due to war. It was the first World Cup that England participated in, having rejoined FIFA after an earlier dispute. Consequently, England was one of the favorites to win the tournament.

The American team wasn't expected to do anything. There were no thriving leagues in the United States and—after being pounded in qualifying by Mexico and in the 1948 Olympics—the team was scrambling to find better players. The makeup of the U.S. national team was much different than it is today, in which every player's full-time job is soccer. The players on the 1948 team all had full-time jobs other than soccer—some were teachers or truck drivers. At the last minute Gaetjens was added to the team, so he was unfamiliar to his own teammates.

But his story was a fascinating one. Gaetjens was born in 1924 in Port-au-Prince, Haiti, to a well-to-do family. His great-grandfather was a German who emigrated to the Caribbean island as a trade representative for the king of Prussia in the mid-nineteenth century. When Joe was born, his father registered his birth certificate at the German embassy in Haiti, in case the child ever wanted to gain German citizenship.

Joe played soccer in Haiti for Etoile Haitienne, which he joined at age fourteen. Playing with the team as a teenager, he won two Haitian championships in

1942 and 1944. But he couldn't make a living playing soccer in Haiti, so his family sent him to study accounting at Columbia University in New York.

There he started playing for a team in the American Soccer League (ASL), Brookhattan. The team was owned by a man who also owned a restaurant called Rudy's. Life was *much* different for professional soccer players back then. There were no multimillion-dollar contracts and endorsement deals. For many players, their soccer salaries weren't enough to make ends meet. Gaetjens supplemented his soccer income by washing dishes in the restaurant.

That's where U.S. Soccer found him. He was leading the ASL in scoring, an athletic player who made acrobatic headers in front of the opposition's goal. According to the rules of the day, a player could represent the United States as long as he promised to pursue citizenship. Gaetjens said he would, so off he went to Brazil with his new team to compete in the 1950 World Cup.

He played all three games for the United States. In the opener against Spain, the Americans took an early lead but gave up three goals in the final nine minutes.

Then came the famous game in the city of Belo

Horizonte. England had the best players in the world and the best league in the world, and they were the heavy favorites. While England was a 3–1 favorite to win the World Cup, the U.S. team's odds were posted at 500–1, meaning oddsmakers predicted it was over 150 times more likely that England would be champions vs. the United States. Even the American coach Bill Jeffrey called his team "sheep ready to be slaughtered."

But Jeffrey's players weren't ready to count themselves out.

"We were confident in that we were playing better than we'd expected," said Walter Bahr, a midfielder on the team, whose two sons—Chris and Matt—would go on to become placekickers in the NFL and win Super Bowl rings. "The game [against Spain] built up our confidence somewhat."

Against England, the Americans were surprised to find support in the stadium. There was a nearby military base, so some American citizens came to watch. But the Brazilians were also cheering for the red, white, and blue. The host fans liked the underdog and were hoping that some team would take out England so Brazil would not have to play them in the final.

As the game went on, more and more fans flocked

to it, perhaps spurred on by the radio broadcast and the unexpected excitement.

In the 37th minute, Bahr took a shot from 25 yards out. It looked to be an easy save for England's goalkeeper Bert Williams, but—out of nowhere—Gaetjens launched himself at the ball, barely connecting with his head, redirecting the shot, and the ball dribbled into the net.

Gaetjens never saw it. His face was planted facedown in the grass. The photographers never saw it. They had surrounded the American goal, convinced all the action would happen there, anticipating a blowout by the English. There is precious little record of the stunning goal. The English journalists insisted it was a mistake. Gaetjens's teammates insisted that it was intentional and emblematic of the way he played.

For the next sixty-three minutes, the English players grew increasingly frustrated as either American keeper Frank Borghi or the goalposts and crossbar kept them from finding the back of the net. Charlie Colombo, a defender from St. Louis, Missouri, stopped a chance by Stan Mortensen, one of England's stars, in the 82nd minute. He was called for a penalty, and the ensuing free kick was blocked by Borghi.

When the victory was complete, Gaetjens was carried off the field by excited fans. Some newspapers published the score in reverse, that England had beaten the United States 1–0. The editors assumed that an operator had simply typed the score wrong. It was an upset for the ages.

England went on to lose to Spain and didn't advance. Neither did the Americans, who lost to Chile. Brazil also had its dreams shattered when it lost to Uruguay in the championship.

But no team was as stunned as England.

"I did feel for them," Bahr said. "For us, it was a victory and we were gonna get our recognition. But how were they going to explain losing that game back home?"

Though some wanted an inquiry because Gaetjens wasn't a citizen, he wasn't the only one. Three players on the U.S. team were citizens of other countries. FIFA launched an investigation, but nothing came of it, because the rules of the time allowed the players to play because they had signed agreements saying they would become citizens.

After the World Cup, Gaetjens went to France, hoping to capitalize on his celebrity. He signed with

Racing Club de France but didn't stay long, injuring his knee after just four games. He moved on to play in a lower French league. But he struggled with knee injuries and returned to Haiti.

There—even though he had been gone for six years—he was welcomed as a conquering hero by a huge crowd at the airport and paraded through the streets. He was famous at home and had some good business opportunities thanks to his celebrity. Because he never followed through with his promise to gain American citizenship, he was eligible to play in a World Cup qualifier for Haiti in 1953. That was his last game.

Gaetjens married and had three children and settled down to a domestic life in Haiti, running a dry cleaners. He wasn't political, but his family was, and they ended up on the losing side of the 1957 election when François Duvalier became the new president. Duvalier evolved into a dictator, declaring himself "president for life," and ordered the execution of many of those who did not support him.

Though Gaetjens tried to stay out of it—and may have thought his celebrity status would save him—he was arrested at his dry cleaners and never heard from again. The assumption is that he was executed in July 1964.

Twelve years later, more than a quarter of a century after he scored the most shocking goal in American soccer history, Joe Gaetjens was inducted into the U.S. Soccer Hall of Fame.

He never became an American citizen. But like so many who have come to these shores, Gaetjens made a significant, positive impact on our society and was part of one of the most improbable tales in our history.

STATISTICS:

Position: forward

Appearances for U.S. national team: 3

Goals for the United States: 1

Appearances for Brookhattan: 64

Goals for Brookhattan: 42

(He also appeared professionally for Haitian and French teams, but statistical records from that era are limited.)

CLAUDIO REYNA

Many of the early American stars on the World Cup teams of the 1990s were the very first in their families to fall in love with soccer.

The parents of several of those players in that first generation didn't know much, if anything, about the sport. Their kids were playing youth soccer, but it wasn't a sport they were familiar with, so they had to read books or ask other people—often those who had grown up in other countries—in order to learn more.

But that wasn't the case for Claudio Reyna. He learned the sport the way many children around the world do: by emulating his parent.

Reyna, who would go on to be one of the most important players in the American program, grew up playing the game with his father, Miguel. Miguel Reyna was a native of Argentina and played professionally for Los Andes, a first-division team in his home country. Miguel and his wife eventually moved to New Jersey and raised a family.

Reyna started to play soccer with his father and older brother when he was a very small child. When the family went to Argentina in the summers, he played there and picked up instincts for the game that many of his American teammates didn't have. He learned to play with an innate feel, rather than only as instructed.

Landon Donovan once said that he learned to be patient by watching Reyna. "I've always been taught to go, go, go. Now I understand rhythm, understand the flow of the game, when you need to go, when you don't need to go, when you shouldn't go. Claudio has that down to an art."

Reyna, a playmaking midfielder, was always the best player on his teams. During Reyna's three years on high school varsity at St. Benedict's, the New Jersey team went undefeated, 65-0. Reyna was a two-time *Parade* magazine high school player of the year and the Gatorade player of the year in 1991. He was highly recruited and went to the University of Virginia to play for Bruce Arena, who would also later be Reyna's coach on the U.S. national team. At Virginia, Reyna won a national championship in each of his three years and won the Hermann Trophy as the nation's top player in 1993.

Reyna earned his first cap with the U.S. national team in January 1994 at age twenty. He had already decided to leave Virginia after just three years, choosing instead to concentrate on preparation for the World Cup with the American team and then to turn professional.

Reyna had grown up with a picture of Diego Maradona and the 1986 championship Argentina team on his bedroom wall. He dreamed of playing not in a Super Bowl or in a World Series but in a World Cup.

"I guess a lot of American kids don't grow up dreaming of playing in the World Cup," Reyna said. "I did, but I really didn't dream of it being played in my own country."

But that was what happened in 1994, a few months after Reyna's debut with the national team. The United States was hosting the World Cup, and Reyna was expected to be a difference maker for his team.

But in June, during a practice, Reyna injured his hamstring. His injury kept him out of the entire World Cup. It was a sign of things to come.

By that time, his talent had already attracted

interest from clubs around the world. A month after the World Cup, he signed a contract with Bayer Leverkusen of the German Bundesliga. Though he stayed there for three years, he had a hard time cracking the first team and was lent to another German club, Wolfsburg. There he received significant playing time and even became captain. In 1999, he was transferred to the Scottish team, the Rangers, where he stayed for two seasons.

As Reyna's club career started to take off, the 1998 World Cup rolled around, and Reyna finally had a chance to play. The Americans opened against Germany, a team fielding players that Reyna knew well from his professional career in the Bundesliga. The U.S. lost that game and the next two, exiting quickly, despite having more experience and depth than in 1994.

In the 2002 World Cup, Reyna was again plagued by injuries—this time it was his quadriceps—and had to sit out the opening victory against Portugal. But he returned to action and played every minute of the remaining four games, and was named to the all-tournament team.

"Everyone recognizes the value he brings to

his team," said Arena, by then Reyna's coach on the national team.

Reyna was the captain on the World Cup team in 2006 and widely respected.

"Everybody loves Claudio," DaMarcus Beasley said. "He's a laid-back, cool guy off the field. On the field, technically he's our best player. He's so smooth, very nonchalant. It looks like he's not working hard, but he is. He's so cool, so calm, so un-frantic."

By the time of the 2006 World Cup in Germany, Reyna was playing for Manchester City, after a stop in Sunderland. Injuries continued to take a toll on his playing time and came back to bite him again in the World Cup. He sprained his knee in what would be the Americans' final game of the tournament, against Ghana, a loss that eliminated the team. The next day Reyna announced his retirement from the national team at age thirty-one.

In 2007, Reyna signed with the New York Red Bulls, his first MLS team. But, again because of injuries, he only played a handful of games. He retired in 2008.

For a time, he served as the U.S. Soccer youth technical director. In 2013, he became the sporting director of the MLS expansion team, New York City FC. Reyna suffered a personal tragedy when his son Jack, the oldest of his four children, died of cancer at age thirteen.

As a kid, Reyna dreamed big when he looked at the picture of Diego Maradona on his bedroom wall. He didn't quite reach Maradona status, but he surpassed what most expected from an American soccer player.

"I would have been happy to play in one World Cup, when I made the first one in 1994," Reyna said when he retired from the national team. "To make four is something beyond my dreams. I would have never thought that growing up."

Reyna helped the U.S. soccer program grow up. He was a pivotal member of the team as it matured and became more respected. During his time with the program, it rose from the twenty-third-ranked team by FIFA to No. 8 in the world.

"When we look down the road to the day where we eventually win a World Cup," Arena said, "Claudio is going to be remembered as one of the greats and one of the pioneers."

STATISTICS:

Position: midfielder

Appearances for U.S. national team: 112

Goals for the United States: 8

Professional appearances (six clubs): 282

Goals for professional clubs: 23

ERIC WYNALDA

n the 1990s, as the Americans were starting to build a soccer tradition and a league, a group of players joined the national team who would go on to become the budding stars of a sport the country was just beginning to learn about.

There was red-bearded and wild-haired Alexi Lalas, a defender, a guitar player, and an outspoken interviewee who became the first American to play in Italy's Serie A. And Tony Meola, the hard-nosed New Jersey goalkeeper who once tried to get an NFL place-kicker job. Ponytailed Marcelo Balboa anchored the team's defense.

They all became recognizable in this country thanks to the 1994 World Cup and the launch of Major League Soccer. But the most important in the group was Eric Wynalda.

Wynalda was the first significant goal scorer for

the modern U.S. team. He still stands at fourth on the all-time scoring list with thirty-four goals in 106 appearances between 1990 and 2000.

Wynalda grew up in Southern California, one of millions of little kids who ran around on a soccer field and ate orange slices.

A hyperactive child who received a diagnosis of dyslexia when he was in junior high, Wynalda struggled in school and had a hard time staying still. He was smart, funny, and quick-witted but not very interested in school.

But when he tagged along with his older brother to a soccer game when he was five, he was fascinated and focused. It was a rare sight.

"So my parents got me a ball," Wynalda said. "And that was it. It was all over."

Suddenly he had an outlet for all of his hyper energy. He used it up on the soccer field, kicking the ball around, trying to get it into the back of the net. The family pediatrician had advised Wynalda's parents to find something he liked and support him, so that's what they did. They ventured all over Southern California to tournaments, went to see North American Soccer League games at the Los Angeles Coliseum, and watched any soccer matches—there weren't many back then—that were available on television in the days before cable.

As an eight-year-old, Wynalda was already making headlines in the local paper after he scored fifty-six goals in a season to lead his team to a state championship. He later played on club teams and for his high school team, where he scored eighty-eight goals in three varsity seasons.

After high school, he went to San Diego State University (SDSU). There he gained a reputation as a difficult player—he called himself "volatile and uncontrollable"—taunting opponents and being a bad sport. Despite his attitude, Wynalda excelled on the field, which led to more opportunities after college. After three years, he turned pro by accepting a $500 fee to play in an exhibition in Brazil, abdicating his final year of eligibility at SDSU.

Around that time, in 1990, the Americans' first World Cup appearance since 1950, Wynalda was the youngest member of the team. He did not have a great debut, earning a red card and being ejected for elbowing a Czechoslovakian player, in a humiliating 5–1 loss. Because of his ejection, he had to sit out the next game, against host Italy. Given his fiery attitude, this wouldn't be the last time his passion would lead to trouble. A couple of years later, he was sent home from camp by the new U.S. coach Bora Milutinović for elbowing a player.

Though the United States had made it back onto the international stage in a major way, during Wynalda's era there were still no significant professional American leagues. With limited options available, he played for the San Francisco Bay Blackhawks, of the American Professional Soccer League, but was eventually released. His coach, Laurie Calloway, cited a lack of commitment by Wynalda.

But being fired from the Blackhawks ended up being a fortunate move for Wynalda. In 1992, U.S. Soccer lent him to FC Saarbrücken in Germany. Wynalda became one of the first Americans to play in the Bundesliga.

Though the German fans were skeptical of Wynalda, he scored nine goals in his first ten games. Because of his California roots, the fans called him "Beach Boy" and chanted his name. The tabloid newspapers were full of stories about him.

When the World Cup came to the United States

in 1994, the members of the American team became more noticed in their own country. Despite his past troubles, Wynalda was a vital part of the team, and his experience in Germany seemed to have helped him mature.

In the team's first game, in Detroit against Switzerland, Wynalda scored on a spectacular 30-yard free kick to even the score 1–1. That goal put the United States in position to advance to the second round, which they did thanks to a shocking win over Colombia.

In the round-of-16 game against Brazil on the Fourth of July, the Americans battled but eventually lost 1–0 to the team that went on to claim the championship.

After the success of the 1994 World Cup, it was clear that America's appetite for soccer was growing. It was time to have a serious professional league in the United States. Wynalda, like the other stars on the 1994 team, was one of the key players who helped launch Major League Soccer in 1996. He was the original franchise player for the San Jose Clash, which eventually became the Earthquakes. On April 6, 1996, Wynalda scored the inaugural goal of the new league in the 88th minute against D.C. United.

Because soccer was new, there was great concern that a scoreless draw in the first match of the league would be a disappointment to Americans who were still learning about the game. Wynalda's goal helped avert any such embarrassment. And it was the start of what would be an excellent season for him, one that would end with Wynalda winning U.S. Soccer Athlete of the Year.

Wynalda's original coach with the Clash, Laurie Calloway, was the same one who had released him from the Blackhawks. Their relationship was turbulent, and Wynalda—by demanding a trade and criticizing coaching decisions—won the battle, with Calloway getting fired.

"I'm a bad politician," Wynalda said. "You ask me a question, I'll give you an honest answer."

Honesty—not his but a teammate's—was an issue in the 1998 World Cup. The American team had qualified for the World Cup in France when captain John Harkes was shockingly released in the middle of preparation. Years later, it was revealed that he was having an inappropriate relationship with Wynalda's wife, whom Wynalda later divorced. The turn of events seemed to rip the American team apart, and they were in chaos in France, finishing dead last in the field of thirty-two.

Despite the embarrassing finish in the World Cup, Wynalda continued to find success in MLS. Yet after three seasons with the San Jose Clash, Wynalda was lent to a Mexican club, but he got injured. Then he returned to MLS when he was traded to the Miami Fusion. He played for two other MLS teams and ended his career in another North American pro soccer league, the United Soccer League's first division, before retiring.

In 2004 Wynalda was elected to the National Soccer Hall of Fame. He worked as a coach and technical director for different minor league teams. One of those amateur teams, Cal FC, made it all the way to the fourth round of the 2012 U.S. Open Cup under Wynalda's guidance.

He also went on to use his quick wit and honesty in broadcasting, first with ESPN and later with Fox Sports. He often used his sharp tongue to criticize the American team during World Cups and qualifying games.

Wynalda was never afraid to speak his mind. Especially about the legacy he helped create.

STATISTICS:

Position: forward

Appearances for U.S. national team: 106

Goals for the United States: 34

Professional appearances: 220

Goals for professional clubs: 64

CLINT DEMPSEY

Clint Dempsey, one of the greatest soccer players the United States has ever produced, is the kind of athlete the American public loves: tough, successful, and brave.

Though Dempsey succeeded playing in Europe, there was always something very American about him. Raised in a hardscrabble Texas town, learning to play the game in adult leagues, he exemplified a gritty, daring kind of American style.

"Clint tries [stuff]," his coach Bruce Arena once said about him.

Dempsey was never tapped to be a star, never groomed as the great American hope. But he became perhaps the greatest goal scorer in American history, and will end up being considered one of the best players the United States has ever produced.

Dempsey grew up in Nacogdoches, a town in

East Texas with a population of 30,000. For much of his childhood his family lived in a trailer in his grandparents' backyard. He learned to play soccer with his brother Ryan, who was five years older. They played in the neighborhood, sometimes on dirt fields, with many of the local kids who were Hispanic immigrants. They watched all the soccer they could on Spanish-language television. As a teenager, Dempsey played in Hispanic adult leagues, with former professional or semipro players.

"Playing with men, you have to learn quickly," Dempsey said. "It's sink or swim. It forced me to develop."

And it taught him an effective style: "Keeping the ball and making the other team work. The Hispanic league was like that."

Beginning in fifth grade, Dempsey started making the six-hour round-trip journey to Dallas three times a week to play with an elite Dallas youth club. In order to allow Dempsey to play, the family sold its boat and held off on any major purchases or vacations. But in 1995, his older sister began getting very good at tennis and the family decided that some financial resources would be shifted from Clint's soccer career to Jennifer's tennis career. But tragically, later that year, when she was just sixteen, Jennifer died of a brain aneurysm.

"When something like that happens, your perspectives change," Ryan Dempsey, Clint's brother, said. "Clint would go out and practice twice as much, work twice as hard. He dedicated everything to her."

Dempsey played for his club in Texas but was lightly recruited for college. He ultimately earned a partial scholarship to Furman, a small private college in South Carolina. He played there from 2001 to 2004. In his three seasons, he led Furman to the National Collegiate Athletic Association (NCAA) tournament twice. It was there that he acquired his nickname "Deuce," which he would also use as his rapper name when he did freestyles. In fact, along with fellow rappers XO and Big Hawk, Dempsey is featured rapping the song "Don't Tread" in a Nike soccer advertising campaign for the 2006 World Cup.

During his time at Furman, the Americans had their best run ever at the World Cup in 2002. Dempsey was intrigued; the young star of the team, Landon Donovan, was just a year older than he was.

"I was nowhere close to being with the national

team at that time," Dempsey said. "I was just a fan like everybody else."

Dempsey had played in his regional Olympic Development Program but wasn't in the national team program until he was tapped to play in the 2003 Under-20 World Cup. His tough attitude was formed from frequently being overlooked and having to fight for all his chances. He made his debut with the senior national team in 2004 against Jamaica in a World Cup qualifier. He made his first World Cup roster in 2006 and was the only American to score a goal in the tournament, against Ghana.

By that time, Dempsey had been drafted by MLS. He was showing signs of the creative, free-roaming player who could drop back into the attack or push forward, often the beneficiary of a broken play or a turnover.

When he was selected in the 2004 draft, he was overshadowed by the top pick, Freddy Adu, who was supposed to be the savior of American soccer. Dempsey's hometown team, Dallas, passed on him twice, with the sixth and seventh picks. Finally, with the eighth pick, the player who actually would be the future of American soccer was selected by the

New England Revolution. In three seasons with New England, Dempsey appeared in seventy-one games. He was the Rookie of the Year in 2004 and scored the game-winning goal in a 2005 playoff semifinal, putting the Revolution in the MLS Cup.

In 2006, the big leagues came calling. British team Fulham offered MLS $4 million for Dempsey, a record for an MLS transfer at the time. Dempsey stayed with Fulham for five and a half seasons, becoming the highest-scoring American to ever play in the Premier League, surpassing Brian McBride, who also played for Fulham. In his first year, his goal against Liverpool late in the season saved Fulham from being demoted to a lower league. Dempsey eventually became Fulham's all-time leading scorer.

Dempsey became more and more important to the fortunes of U.S. Soccer. In the 2010 World Cup cycle he was a key player. In the Confederations Cup in 2009, he scored in the team's 2–0 upset of Spain and also scored against Brazil. He received the Bronze Ball as the third-best performer in the tournament.

In South Africa at the 2010 World Cup, Dempsey scored against England, a soft shot that was misplayed by the English goalkeeper. He appeared to score again against Algeria, but in a controversial call, he was ruled offsides, though replays appeared to show otherwise.

During his tenure with the American team, Dempsey had formed a bond with Landon Donovan, their chemistry apparent on the field. But Donovan was left off the 2014 World Cup team. In the first game, Jozy Altidore was hurt. With two of their stars out, it was time for Dempsey to step up. Most of the scoring responsibility fell to him.

Under pressure, he delivered.

Wearing the captain's armband, he scored just twenty-nine seconds into the first match against Ghana, the quickest American goal in World Cup history. In doing so, Dempsey became the first American to score in three different World Cups. He also scored in the team's draw against Portugal.

Dempsey was a creative, fascinating player, breaking the mold of American players who were somewhat predictable. He could also be unpredictable in other ways, occasionally getting in fights with opponents, once tearing up a referee's notebook in a rage—an incident that led to a two-year ban from the U.S. Open Cup—and receiving the occasional red card.

In 2012, Fulham's all-time scorer left to sign

a contract with Tottenham Hotspur. The deal, a $9.5 million transfer fee, ended up making Dempsey the highest-paid American soccer player in history. In his single season there, he scored seven goals.

In 2013, Dempsey decided he was ready to return to his homeland after seven years. He signed a huge deal with the Seattle Sounders. Though he went back to Fulham briefly on a loan, Dempsey settled back into MLS as he prepared for the 2014 World Cup.

In 2016, Dempsey was given a diagnosis of an irregular heartbeat, ending his season with the Sounders and sidelining him from the U.S. national team as it attempted to qualify for the 2018 World Cup. There were concerns about whether he would be able to continue with his dazzling career.

But, ever resilient, he returned. During his nine-month absence from the national team, coach Jürgen Klinsmann was fired and replaced by Bruce Arena, the first coach who had called Dempsey into camp back in 2004. The Americans were at the bottom of their qualifying group. In his first game back, against Honduras in March 2017, Arena asked Dempsey how many minutes he could play, and Dempsey told him as many as was needed.

He scored a hat trick.

"I'm a fighter," he said. "I looked for the opportunity to show that I should still be out there."

After that game, he acknowledged the emotion of the moment.

"You're just grateful for every game you get to play in because you never know when it's going to be taken from you," he said. "There's always the possibility that you're not going to be able to come back and be at that high level."

A few months later, in the Gold Cup final, Dempsey scored a goal that tied him with Landon Donovan as the team's all-time leading scorer. But his magic ran out: in the Americans' last-gasp attempt at qualifying for the 2018 World Cup, Dempsey had a late-game shot that hit the post. An inch in the other direction and he would have been in his fourth World Cup.

Dempsey was the star who was never groomed for stardom, the kid from a small town in Texas who conquered the Premier League, the surprising, gritty phenom of American soccer.

"Not everything has been cupcakes and ice cream and happy endings," Dempsey said. "It's been a grind. It's been tough. But that's what's made me who I am."

STATISTICS*:

Position: forward

Appearances for U.S. national team: 137

Goals for the United States: 57

Professional appearances: 390

Goals for professional clubs: 128

*currently active player

MICHAEL BRADLEY

I t happens in every sport. When a son follows in the footsteps of his father, he has to prove himself on his own.

When a son ends up being coached by his father, he ends up facing accusations of nepotism. That he is only getting a chance to play because of his bloodlines.

That was the story for Michael Bradley, when he was coming up with the U.S. national team. He emerged as a force while his father, Bob, was the national team coach.

But Bradley proved his worth on his own, continuing to play for the team and contributing long after his father had moved on.

"Obviously there have always been advantages and disadvantages for having my dad be a coach," Michael said once. "But it has never got in the way of what I'm trying to do.

"He taught me how to act, how to carry myself, and taught me that if I came in to training every day and gave everything I had to the team, that people on the inside would respect that."

Soccer dictated the details of Bradley's life from the start. He was born in Princeton, New Jersey, where his father was the coach of the Princeton college program. When Michael was a teenager, his dad became the head coach of the MLS Chicago Fire and the family moved to Illinois. There, Bradley played on the Sockers FC, one of the top youth clubs. When he was fifteen, he went to the residential training academy in Bradenton, Florida, that was affiliated with U.S. Soccer, where he stayed for two years.

With soccer in his blood and top-notch resources at his disposal, Bradley quickly developed into a talented player. He turned professional at just sixteen years old and was drafted by the MetroStars of MLS. But it was no ordinary draft pick. Bradley was drafted by his father, who had moved on from the Fire to coach the MetroStars. The rumblings of nepotism started right away in Bradley's professional career.

He didn't play at all as a rookie but became a starter in his second year. That same year, his father was fired as head coach before the season ended. After the firing, Bradley scored his first-ever MLS goal on a header. It was an awkward situation, the kind to which he would become accustomed.

Following that season, he was transferred to the Dutch club Heerenveen, becoming the youngest MLS player ever to be sold. In 2006, at just nineteen, he found success in the Netherlands. Eventually, he became a starter and a reliable goal scorer in the attack.

That year, 2006, was a momentous one for the Bradley family. Michael was brought in to the national team pre–World Cup training camp by coach Bruce Arena. Arena had known Bradley since he was a baby—Bob Bradley had been Arena's assistant coach at University of Virginia before Michael was even born.

Though he didn't make the final roster, Bradley got his first start in a pre–World Cup friendly match. After the American men disappointed fans by not advancing to the second round, Arena's contract was not renewed. The federation was interested in hiring German Jürgen Klinsmann but didn't get a deal done, and Bob Bradley was named interim coach.

The next May, the interim title was removed and

Bob Bradley became the full-time head coach of the U.S. team. By that time, his son was an established member of the player pool, playing as defensive midfielder. Though he showed immaturity at times as a young player—getting sent off for a late tackle in the Gold Cup—he began producing.

Bradley had a knack for coming up with a big goal in a big game. In 2009, in a qualifying match for the 2010 World Cup, he opened eyes by scoring both goals for the U.S. team in a victory over Mexico in Columbus, Ohio. Later that year, in the 2009 Confederations Cup, Bradley played well but was sent off late in the team's upset win against Spain because of a rough tackle and was forced to miss the final against Brazil. Some wondered if he had an attitude problem and if, because his father was his coach, it was being ignored.

But in the 2010 World Cup in South Africa, Bradley was an instrumental player for the American team, starting all four games and scoring the second goal in a critical draw with Slovenia. He began shedding the perception that he was immature and that he was only getting a chance to play because of his father.

All along, Bradley continued to prove him-self in Europe, away from his father's influence. He signed a four-year deal with German team Borussia Mönchengladbach of the Bundesliga in 2008. In 2011 he was lent to Aston Villa in the Premier League. Later he moved to Serie A in Italy, playing for both Chievo and Roma.

Though Bob Bradley was rehired to coach the U.S. team through the next World Cup cycle, he was abruptly fired in July 2011 following the team's Gold Cup final loss to Mexico by a score of 4–2. Bradley faced criticism that his style was too bland and that he was too loyal to certain players, including his son.

"In soccer, in life, you learn to deal with things that are difficult," Michael Bradley said at the time. "You learn to deal with things that don't go your way or that are difficult for people close to you. This is not different. It's part of the game."

While his father moved on to coach the Egyptian national team, and then clubs in Norway, France, and Swansea of the Premier League, Bradley continued to be an integral part of the American effort. Klinsmann kept him as a starter at midfield, proof that Bradley's worth had nothing to do with favoritism.

In the 2014 World Cup, Bradley played all 390 minutes of the Americans' stay in the tournament. His brilliant assist set up Julian Green's goal in the overtime loss to Belgium. In 2015 he earned his 100th cap with the U.S. national team. By that time, Bradley had returned to North America to play with MLS team Toronto FC.

In late 2016, Klinsmann was fired and Arena—the coach who had called Bradley into his first national team camp—was back. Arena relied heavily on Bradley as the U.S. team tried to dig itself out of a hole in qualifying for the 2018 World Cup.

A big moment in that effort came in Azteca Stadium in Mexico City, a place where the American men had never won a qualifying game and rarely scored a goal. Just six minutes in, Bradley intercepted a poor pass from Mexican star Chicharito, sprinted forward, and chipped the ball in from 35 yards out, stunning the Mexican team and their enthusiastic fans. It was hailed as one of the most beautiful goals in American soccer history.

Mexico came back to tie the game, but escaping Azteca with a crucial qualifying point was huge for the Americans.

Bradley, by now the team captain, again showed savvy and poise in a big game.

"We knew in certain moments that Chicharito was looking to come to the ball," Bradley said. "I felt like I was able to read what he wanted to do and step in. It led to a good goal for us."

With Bradley as the captain, the U.S. men went on to win the Gold Cup in the summer of 2017. As Arena brought young players into the mix, pairing some with Bradley in the midfield, Bradley provided a calm, veteran presence.

"He's demonstrated great leadership," Arena said. "If you know Michael Bradley, you know that everything is important to Michael. He's very serious, professional, focused."

But the U.S. team failed to qualify for the 2018 World Cup, one of the biggest disappointments of Bradley's career.

During his career, Bradley had evolved into the leader of the U.S. team. Not because of his father or because of any outside forces. But because of his own hard work and talent.

STATISTICS*:

Position: midfielder

Appearances for U.S. national team: 136

Goals for the United States: 17

Professional appearances (seven clubs): 367

Goals for professional clubs: 44

*currently active player

JOZY ALTIDORE

From the moment Jozy Altidore burst on the scene as a sixteen-year-old, he was supposed to be "the next big thing" for American soccer.

Such expectations have overwhelmed the careers of other young players, like Freddy Adu, who was tapped to be the savior American soccer needed years earlier. Adu never came close to meeting those astronomical expectations, and at times it has looked like the burden might prove too much for Altidore as well.

But despite injuries, constant scrutiny, and those heavy expectations, Altidore put together a solid career that continued through three World Cup cycles. He climbed the charts for the national team as the third all-time goal scorer in history, behind Landon Donovan and the player he was often paired with in the American attack, Clint Dempsey.

Altidore was born in New Jersey and raised in

Florida. His parents were immigrants from Haiti. Altidore grew up playing youth soccer in Florida and joined the under-17 residential training academy in Bradenton.

"I don't think I'd be where I am without [the training academy]," Altidore said. "It helped bridge the gap. Having the ability to train every day with the best players available at the time pushed me to be better. It was very valuable for me in learning how to be a pro."

And train him to be a pro, it did. Altidore was drafted by the MetroStars (which became the Red Bulls that season) in the 2006 MLS SuperDraft when he was just sixteen. He missed much of that season because he was working on his high school diploma. He made his pro debut in August 2006 and scored his first goal a month later. While with the Red Bulls, he became the youngest player ever to start a game and score a goal in MLS history.

Being so young, Altidore's experiences early on differed from his teammates'. For example, his mother moved with him to New Jersey and drove him to practices because Altidore didn't have his driver's license yet. In May 2007, he had to get permission from then-coach Bruce Arena to miss a game so that he could take his girlfriend to her high school prom.

When Altidore walked on the field, though, he wasn't a boy among men but a gifted player with great potential. That year he led the U.S. team at the Under-20 World Cup and made his senior team debut. He scored his first goal for the national team in February 2008.

Later that year, Villareal of La Liga signed Altidore for $10 million, at the time the largest transfer fee paid for a MLS player. He made his debut in September, and in November he became the first American to score in La Liga. In early 2009, Villareal lent Altidore to Xerez, a second-division team, but because of an injury, he never played. Later that year, he was lent to Hull City of the Premier League. Then two years later, he was lent to Bursaspor in Turkey.

During that time, Altidore—still a teenager—was creating excitement with the national team. He scored a hat trick against Trinidad and Tobago during qualifying, becoming the youngest American to do so. He played for the American team in the 2008 Olympics, the last men's Olympic team the United States fielded. He scored an away goal against El Salvador. At the

Confederations Cup, he scored a goal in an upset victory over Spain.

The expectations were at a high point and the next year, Altidore started at striker in all four of the United States' games in the 2010 World Cup. But he didn't score at all and had just one assist. Around that time, people started to criticize him, saying that he wasn't living up to the hype.

By that point, Altidore had scored just six goals in the three years he'd spent playing for international clubs. The fear was very real that he simply couldn't distinguish himself among the competition.

That changed in 2011 when Altidore signed with the Dutch club AZ. In his first season he scored twenty goals. In his second, he scored thirty-one, breaking Clint Dempsey's record for the most goals scored by an American in a European club season. He helped AZ win the Dutch KNVB Cup for the first time in thirty-one years.

Altidore had finally found success in Europe. But playing there came with complications. As a black man, he suffered through racist chants from Dutch fans. It was among the worst abuse he'd ever been subjected to on the field.

"It's a bit disappointing that these things still happen in this time that we're in," Altidore told TV station Eredivisie Live. "But what are you going to do? You just hope these people can find a way to improve themselves. You can only pray for them."

Altidore was later asked to join a FIFA task force on racism in soccer.

"Racism in football is not a little problem," Altidore said. "It's a big problem, a problem that is more alive than people realize."

After Altidore's success in the Netherlands, AZ sold his contract to Sunderland in the Premier League. After a fast start, Altidore's scoring and playing time tapered off. Looking for a place where he would get more playing time, he returned to MLS, to Toronto FC, where he played alongside longtime USA teammate Michael Bradley.

Though Altidore found success briefly in Europe, his performances with the national team were erratic. He suffered a serious hamstring injury in the 2011 Gold Cup, and following that setback, he had an almost two-year scoring drought between 2011 and 2013. But then he set an American record, scoring in five consecutive games. Altidore seemed to be clicking in the lead up to the 2014 World Cup, where he was expected to be a factor. But in the Americans' first game against Ghana, Altidore pulled his hamstring and had to be carried off the field. He didn't play again in the World Cup.

It was another case of Altidore, through no fault of his own, not meeting the expectations placed on his shoulders.

Yet once he recovered from his injury, Altidore continued to play a key role under American coach Jürgen Klinsmann, scoring fourteen goals between fall 2014 and fall 2016. When Arena returned as coach of the national team in 2016, he continued to rely on Altidore, who had steadily moved up the American goal-scoring chart to third place overall.

Altidore was paired at times with Clint Dempsey on the Gold Cup roster in the summer of 2017, and the American duo found a scoring touch. It was a combination they had hoped would be at work in the 2014 World Cup.

"I think their skills complement each other, their mentality complements each other," Arena said.

That was obvious in the semifinal of the Gold Cup against Costa Rica, when Dempsey came on as a substitute and immediately made a perfect assist to

Altidore, who buried the ball for a goal. In the final against Jamaica, Altidore hit a curling free kick to give the United States the lead. The team went on to win the Gold Cup, part of a resurgent effort under Arena as it tried to qualify for the 2018 World Cup. For Altidore, it was a triumphant signal to critics that he was a serious competitor.

Altidore, who had become a father and enjoyed living in North America, said he was in a good place.

Part of that positive attitude had nothing to do with soccer. Throughout his career, Altidore was active in charity causes, including providing scholarships, clean water, and hurricane and earthquake relief money for Haiti, the impoverished land his parents had fled many years earlier. Altidore has been part of aid missions and also helped fund a program to bring television watch parties to Haiti during the Copa America soccer tournament, so that Haitians, many of whom couldn't afford a TV, could watch their team.

"I'm just happy," he said after his Gold Cup victory. "I'm enjoying my soccer, enjoying my life off the field and that's the biggest thing for me."

But the American team failed to qualify for the 2018

World Cup. Though some of his longtime teammates would retire after the failed campaign, Altidore—just twenty-eight—could carry on his career into the next cycle. The heavy expectations he arrived with were no longer weighing him down.

STATISTICS*:

Position: forward

Appearances for U.S. national team: 107

Goals for the United States: 39

Professional appearances: 324

Goals for professional clubs: 114

*currently active player

BRAD FRIEDEL

The first American soccer players to gain respect internationally were goalkeepers. And, of those, Brad Friedel was one of the best of them all.

Unlike their teammates, American goalkeepers were noticed. They were respected. They were very good. They became the first soccer players to start to change the impression that Americans couldn't play the sport at the highest levels.

One theory for why the United States has consistently turned out solid goalkeepers is that the country's best athletes grow up playing other sports, using their hands, developing eye-hand coordination, and jumping and leaping to catch things. That happens in baseball, football, and basketball. Often, tall athletes with good leaping ability were recruited from other sports and put into goal.

Friedel was no exception. Growing up in Ohio, he

was a multisport athlete, playing tennis, basketball, and soccer and exceling at all three. He was an Ohio All-State basketball player. He was spotted by UCLA coaches at a soccer tournament and recruited.

"Brad is the one and only player I ever flew out during my season to watch play," said then–UCLA coach Sigi Schmid. "It took me that one time, plus what [my assistants] had said, that made me realize there was something special about him."

At UCLA, Friedel was invited to try out for the famed Bruins basketball team. He opted to stick with soccer instead, trying to constantly get better, and was in goal when the Bruins won a national championship in 1990. He won the Hermann Trophy as the nation's top soccer player in 1993. He also played for the U.S. U-23 team at the Barcelona Olympics, where he was spotted by a coach from British club team Nottingham Forest.

With that connection in hand, Friedel left UCLA a year early for a professional career, hoping to land with Nottingham Forest. He was unsuccessful and tried for years to get to England or Scotland but was continuously denied a work permit to play in either country. He spent time with a Norwegian team but never played.

The years passed, and because of these complications, Friedel struggled to find an opportunity that would result in real playing time. Resigned, he returned to the United States, then headed to Turkey to play. In 1997, he signed with the Columbus Crew of MLS in his home state of Ohio. He quickly found the success he'd been denied abroad. That season he was named MLS goalkeeper of the year.

"He completely changed the culture of our club, the locker room, training, on and off the field, when he joined us," said Greg Andrulis, who coached the Crew. "Suddenly we had a world-class player in our midst. The team was better and the league was better because Brad was in it."

But Friedel still wanted to play overseas. His stay in MLS only lasted one season, before he headed to famed Premier League club Liverpool.

Despite his talent, Friedel had to wait his turn with the United States national team as well. He earned his first cap with the senior team in 1992. But he lost out on the starting job for the 1994 World Cup team to Tony Meola, making the team as a backup. Friedel was again the backup in the 1998 World Cup, to Kasey Keller. But with the U.S. team in an 0–2 hole, he got his chance to start a World Cup game against Yugoslavia in the final game of group play. He gave up a goal in the third minute—the only goal of the game. Friedel also was a member of the 2000 Olympic team in Australia, as one of the older players allowed on the U-23 team.

By that time, Friedel had finally started to realize his dream of playing in Europe. He had his visa request approved in late 1997. He stayed with Liverpool for three seasons but only played sparingly. He was signed by another English team, Blackburn, in late 2000, and that is where his career truly began to take off. At the time of his signing, Blackburn was in the second division, but Friedel's performance in goal helped the team's promotion back to the Premier League's top division. In the 2002–2003 season, he recorded fifteen clean sheets, earning his team's Player of the Year award.

Friedel is proud of his role as a groundbreaking American player in Europe.

"All of us back then, we all helped pave the way for the guys who are playing now," he said.

Friedel carried that newfound confidence into his position with the national team. In the 2002 World Cup, he was, at last, the starting goalkeeper as the

Americans made their best-ever run to the quarter-finals. He started all five games and was dubbed "the human wall," becoming the first World Cup goalkeeper in twenty-eight years to save two penalty kicks, one against South Korea and one against Poland.

It was a phenomenal performance. And it was the pinnacle of Friedel's national team career. If he hadn't come of age in a time when the U.S. team was rich in goalkeepers, he might have had more opportunities and been even more dominant.

He was a great shot-stopper, using his huge wingspan to his advantage.

"He's in the elite," Schmid said. "The U.S. is blessed that they had a really good run of goalkeepers with Keller, Meola, and Friedel—all in the same era. For me, Brad was always the guy who had more of the complete package. He is in the top ten of U.S. players all-time."

Friedel retired from the national team in 2005, at age thirty-three, with eighty-two appearances under his belt. Because he was committed to his career in England, the back-and-forth travel to the United States for qualifying games and friendlies took its toll, and he decided he'd had enough of international play.

But he was nowhere near finished with his playing career. After eight seasons in Blackburn, in 2008 Friedel signed a three-year contract with Aston Villa. In 2011, he signed with Tottenham. He was a starter until October 2012, when he was a backup for a game. That ended his record for most consecutive games played by a Premier League player, at an astonishing 310, dating back to 2004.

Friedel finally retired from his professional career in 2015 at age forty-three. He credited his longevity, in part, to daily yoga, which kept him flexible. He was the oldest player to play for both Aston Villa and Tottenham.

"It's amazing that it has transpired like this," he said near the end of his career.

Beginning in 2015, Friedel was the head coach of the U.S. under-19 team, helping to develop talent headed toward the national team.

"We're in a pretty solid place," he said in 2017, shortly before becoming head coach of MLS' New England Revolution.

He is helping to find and encourage the talent that will take American soccer into the future—a future that Friedel and his long, distinguished career helped create.

STATISTICS:

Position: goalkeeper

Appearances for U.S. national team: 82

Shutouts for U.S. national team: 24

Professional appearances (six clubs): 668

Shutouts for professional clubs: 132

PAUL CALIGIURI

For decades, the United States wasn't invited to the world's biggest party. Every four years, nations got together, flags were flown, fans celebrated, and soccer was played. The party was always colorful, diverse, and fun, and millions of people adored it.

But the Americans didn't go to the World Cup party. The U.S. team didn't qualify after 1950. The Americans never played in the same tournament as Pelé. When their neighbors to the south, Mexico, hosted the World Cup twice—in 1970 and 1986—the United States was left out.

During these disappointing years, there were still small pockets of rabid soccer fans throughout the United States. There was brief but intense interest in the sport when Pelé came to play in the North American Soccer League. But that league folded, interest waned, and soccer in the United States was pretty much relegated to something children did on the weekends.

Paul Caligiuri changed all that.

In 1989 he scored a goal that was dubbed "the shot heard 'round the world," a goal that helped launch a soccer movement in the United States.

Caligiuri was one of those children playing soccer on the weekend. He grew up in Diamond Bar, a small city near Los Angeles. When he was seven, in 1971, he was riding his bike and ran into some friends who were signing up for a youth soccer league. Paul decided to sign up too.

He became obsessed with the sport, practicing shooting for hours in his driveway, playing on all-star teams, and eventually starring on his high school squad. He played at UCLA and was the captain on a team that won the collegiate national championship in 1985.

After graduating he played on a semiprofessional team, the San Diego Nomads. He caught a break when he was invited to play in an exhibition at the Rose Bowl, following the 1986 World Cup in Mexico, between the European All-Stars and the Rest of the World. Caligiuri was the token Southern California player, invited as a nice gesture. Whatever the reason,

Caligiuri took advantage of the opportunity. He made a pass that caught the eye of a German, Felix Magath, who persuaded his team, Hamburger SV, to take a look at Caligiuri.

Caligiuri had a tryout, signed a contract, and became the first American-born player to sign with the prestigious Bundesliga.

"It was an opportunity to play at a higher level and I grabbed at it," he said. "I didn't want to leave California. But I knew what I had to do to become a better player."

He was transferred by Hamburg during his time in Germany, and got a contract with a second-division team in West Germany. He moved around to other German teams over the next few years, winning an East German championship with FC Hansa Rostock.

In 1989, he returned home to try to help the United States qualify for the 1990 World Cup. Some of the other players—all former or current college players—on the team resented or were jealous of Caligiuri, who wasn't shy about sharing his newfound knowledge. Eventually the team had to hold a players-only meeting to clear the air before the final qualifying game in Port of Spain, Trinidad.

SECOND HALF: PAUL CALIGIURI •

There was a lot at stake in the game on November 19, 1989. The United States had to beat Trinidad and Tobago to make it to its first World Cup in forty years. A tie or a loss would send T&T through. There was a window of opportunity in the region because Mexico was in the midst of a two-year ban. In previous qualifications for the past nine World Cups, the American team usually hadn't made it out of the first round.

Though Caligiuri had been ineffective in his first few games since returning to the team, coach Bob Gansler made the decision to start him in midfield against T&T, with the instructions to not go forward, but to lie back and defend. That Caligiuri ignored those instructions at a pivotal moment was not a shock.

"One thing that Paul Caligiuri never had was a lack of confidence in his own ability," Gansler said. "Paul would do audacious things."

Thirty minutes into the first half, Caligiuri received a pass from Tab Ramos at midfield. The ball bounced off his chest, and Caligiuri caught up with it, chipping the ball around his defender with his right foot. And then—from a whopping 30 yards out and still on the run—he hammered a left-footed shot, which curved

197

into the top right corner of the net, over Trinidadian goalkeeper Michael Maurice.

It was a beautiful goal. And a bold stroke.

Rob Hughes, one of the top soccer writers in the world, wrote, "Pelé would have had a pop at goal from here. Maradona probably would. A handful of Europe's top professionals might contemplate it."

Instead, it was Caligiuri, the American youth soccer product from Diamond Bar.

The Americans held off their opponent for the rest of the game and, stunningly, had booked their passage to the World Cup in Italy the next summer.

"It was like it was meant to be," said goalkeeper Tony Meola, who earned the shutout.

At the end of the game, the players dogpiled on each other on the field. But the celebration may have been even more intense for U.S. Soccer Federation officials, who were in charge of American soccer.

Sixteen months earlier, on July 4, 1988, the United States had been awarded the 1994 World Cup. The world soccer community was outraged at what was clearly a blatant business decision: FIFA wanted to tap the huge American market despite the U.S. team's poor performances over the past few decades.

To the legions of critics, it was bad enough that the American public and media didn't seem to care at all about soccer. It would have been even more embarrassing if the Americans had never qualified on their own for a modern World Cup (they were entitled to an automatic bid as hosts in 1994).

The American players had heard rumors before the game against T&T that if they didn't come through with a win, the World Cup would be moved to a different location, that the U.S. program might be disbanded. They all felt pressure, real or imagined.

Caligiuri's goal relieved that pressure. And it assured the United States of at least some World Cup experience before they served as hosts four years later.

The taste of victory in the qualifiers was sweet but proved to be short-lived. It wasn't a pretty experience in Italy the next summer for the U.S. team. It was embarrassed, 5–1, in its 1990 World Cup opener in Florence against Czechoslovakia—Caligiuri scored the only goal. The team also lost to host Italy and to Austria. The experience lasted just nine days.

But the American soccer world had changed. Caligiuri went back to Germany, and several of his teammates got the chance to play in Europe as well.

They continued to build the U.S. national team as it prepared for the spotlight of the 1994 World Cup. Caligiuri started every game in that tournament, including a group stage victory over Colombia played at the Rose Bowl, the very stadium where his international career began. The United States went 1–1–1 in group stage and advanced to the knockout round, where it lost to Brazil. Despite the skepticism, the U.S. World Cup was a huge success, drawing record crowds. Gone were the days of embarrassing American soccer.

In an ironic turn of events, the American team's streak of World Cup appearances ended in Trinidad and Tobago in October of 2017, in the same country where the renaissance had begun. The team was eliminated on the last day of qualifying for Russia 2018.

When Major League Soccer was launched, Caligiuri was allocated to the Columbus Crew. The next season he finally returned to California and joined the Los Angeles Galaxy. He played there until he retired.

In retirement he coached both the men's and women's teams at California State Polytechnic University, Pomona for a time and also coached youth teams in Orange County, California. These were young soccer players who were growing up in a different American soccer world, in large part thanks to Caligiuri's goal

"To me it was the most important goal in U.S. history," said his former teammate John Harkes.

Without that goal, without that win, could the worst-case scenario have come true? Could the national team have lost funding? Could the World Cup have been moved? Could Major League Soccer never have been launched?

"It's fascinating to see how far we've come," Caligiuri said. "And to think—what if? If that had never happened, where would we be?"

STATISTICS:

Position: midfielder

Appearances for U.S. national team: 110

Goals for the United States: 5

Professional appearances: 271

Goals for professional clubs: 14

CHRISTIAN PULISIC

C an a teenager who has never even played in a World Cup be one of the United States soccer team's most important eleven?

Yes. That's how electric and significant Christian Pulisic is. And his importance has only grown in the wake of the U.S. men's team's elimination from the 2018 World Cup.

After just twenty appearances on the U.S. national team, only thirteen as a starter, Pulisic was already being called the most-skilled player America had ever produced, a generational talent and the greatest hope for the future.

"He's perhaps the first American superstar in this sport," his former coach Bruce Arena said on television shortly after the player had turned nineteen. "He's a very talented young man."

When the Americans were eliminated from the

chance to play in the 2018 World Cup in Russia on that October night in Couva, Trinidad and Tobago, in 2017 Pulisic wept. Also heartbroken were the millions of fans who had wanted to see the young star in action on soccer's biggest stage.

They are sure to get a chance in the next World Cup cycle.

Pulisic was born in Hershey, Pennsylvania, just three months after the U.S. men's team had an embarrassing outing at the 1998 French World Cup, where the Americans finished last and in disarray. Two decades later, U.S. Soccer is looking to him to pull it out of its latest embarrassment.

Pulisic's parents, Kelley and Mark, both played collegiate soccer at George Mason University. Kelley started playing when she was five years old, and, like many females of her generation, started out playing on a boys' team because there weren't options for girls. In high school and on her club team she was teammates with future women's soccer legend Mia Hamm. Kelley, a defender with an ability to score, eventually earned a scholarship to George Mason University.

While she was there, she met Mark, who played with her older brother on the men's team. Mark's father was from Croatia, and he grew up with a love of European soccer. After graduation, Mark played eight years for the Harrisburg Heat, a Pennsylvania-based indoor soccer team, before becoming a coach.

Pulisic, like his two older siblings, grew up playing a variety of sports. His parents didn't want to push him into soccer, but he kept coming back to it on his own. He was a huge fan of Luis Figo, the Portuguese star who played with Real Madrid; his father still calls him by the nickname "Figo."

When Christian was seven, Kelley received a grant to teach in England for a year. Christian played soccer there and in Detroit, where the family lived after returning to the United States. When the family returned to Pennsylvania, Christian played for a U.S. Soccer Development Academy team. When he was just fourteen, he joined the United States under-17 residency program in Bradenton, Florida.

During the 2014 World Cup, Christian was just another fan, watching the games in his cousin's basement, decked out in U.S. Soccer gear.

"I remember how much it meant to me, being an American," he said. "Obviously I had ambitions to play for the national team."

Borussia Dortmund, a German club with a knack for finding young jewels, was scouting another young American at a tournament in 2014 when it stumbled upon Pulisic. He joined the Bundesliga club's U-17 team in February of 2015. He applied for and received a Croatian passport, based on the citizenship of his grandfather, who was born in Croatia. That helped Pulisic gain a work permit. But when he was approached about playing for Croatia, Christian declined.

His father, Mark, went to Germany with him to help him get settled. He began attending a German high school. After playing with both Dortmund's U-17 and U-19 teams for a year, he was called up to the senior team on the winter break and began playing with it in January of 2016. He got his first start in February. He also got chances in Champions League games, coming off the bench against Real Madrid a few days after his eighteenth birthday, unafraid of superstars Cristiano Ronaldo or Gareth Bale, to assist on the equalizing goal.

Though he missed home, and things like tacos, he learned to speak fluent German and fell in love with his black-and-yellow-clad fans and the working-class city.

"The whole city, how passionate our fans are," he said. "True love [the team slogan] just really shows everything about the club and how much football means to them and how much they mean to us."

Dortmund packs 80,000—the highest average attendance in the world—into the stands. Pulisic didn't seem fazed by fans chanting his name or hounding him for autographs and selfies.

When he was seventeen, he flew home to Pennsylvania from national team training for his senior prom at Hershey High, splurging on a private plane to make the event that is a milestone for every teenager. The next morning, he flew to Kansas City to score his first international goal against Bolivia, coming in as a substitute in his third national team game. He became the youngest American in the modern era to score.

"It was pretty special," Pulisic said of that whirl-wind weekend.

A few months later he made his first start for the national team in a game in Florida. Just days later, he turned eighteen (and celebrated by attending a Justin Bieber concert). He quickly became a fixture in the starting lineup as the United States tried desperately to qualify for the 2018 World Cup. He also quickly became a favorite among American fans looking for the next big thing.

"They're looking for the next star, the next player to be the face of U.S. Soccer," Christian said, adding that that sort of talk was the stuff he hears every day.

When asked how he handles it, he noted, "I try to keep it out of mind. I put enough pressure on myself."

The five-foot-eight midfielder—described as shy but confident, and a perfectionist—became a regular scorer, with nine goals in eighteen games. Even to the untrained eye, his skill level was obvious: incredible speed, passing ability, ways to beat a defense, and intelligence.

"First of all, you don't think he's an American," Arena said.

By mid-2017 other big-time European clubs were inquiring about Christian. He had sponsorship deals with Nike, Gatorade, and Hershey's chocolate. He had changed both the expectations and the storyline for what it means to be an American soccer player.

But as Pulisic ascended, his national team was in turmoil. He went through two coaches—both Jurgen Klinsmann and Arena were fired—during his first eighteen months on the team. And not making the World Cup was a devastating disappointment.

But Pulisic's star will continue to rise in Europe. And as other players move on and the national team is remade, he will shoulder a huge responsibility for the future of American soccer.

He's ready for it.

"The biggest thing my dad taught me was to play without fear," Christian said. "I have done that my whole career. And if I continue to do that, then, he tells me, the sky is the limit."

The sky is the limit for Pulisic. And American soccer hopes he will bring it along with him.

STATISTICS*:

Position: midfielder

Appearances with U.S. national team (as of October 2017): 20

Goals: 9

Appearances with Dortmund (as of October 2017): 48

Goals with Dortmund: 7

*currently active player

TOP TEN BEST SAVES IN WORLD CUP HISTORY

10. KEYLOR NAVAS, COSTA RICA VS. GREECE, 2014, ROUND OF 16

Navas's brilliance against Greece in the knockout round put Costa Rica into the quarterfinals for the first time in history. Navas stopped shot after shot, and for a time it looked like his brilliant effort wouldn't require penalty kicks. But the Greeks tied the game, 1–1, against a short-handed Costa Rica squad and the game went to penalty kicks. Navas, the Man of the Match, made a brilliant one-handed save on a penalty kick to advance Costa Rica.

9. TIM HOWARD, USA VS. BELGIUM, 2014, ROUND OF 16

The 2014 World Cup was a very good one for goalkeepers. Even though the greatest of them all was Germany's Manuel Neuer, others shone on soccer's biggest stage.

Howard set a World Cup record with sixteen saves in a tense knockout round game against highly favored Belgium. The twelfth save was against Vincent Kompany, who received the ball right in front of the net, but a charging Howard knocked it away. He was finally bested by sub Romelu Lukaku, who managed to get one in the net, though three of Howard's final four saves came against the speedy forward.

8. DINO ZOFF, ITALY VS. BRAZIL, 1982, SECOND ROUND

The winner of this game went directly into the semifinals. One of the more entertaining games in World Cup history between two heavyweights, it is usually remembered for Paolo Rossi's hat trick. But it was Italian goalkeeper Dino Zoff's save on a header by Brazilian Zico that preserved Italy's victory. Not only did Zoff stop the shot, but he fell to the ground to gather it up before the ball crossed the line. Italy would go on to win the World Cup.

7. **OLIVER KAHN**, GERMANY VS. USA, 2002,
QUARTERFINALS

Without this save, the most improbable
World Cup scenario might have unfolded:
the Americans could have advanced to
the semifinals of the World Cup. But
Kahn stopped a point-blank shot by
Landon Donovan with his fingertips, the
second save he'd made against the fearless American youngster. The improbable
didn't happen and Germany advanced to
the semifinals.

6. **GUILLERMO OCHOA**, MEXICO VS. BRAZIL, 2014,
GROUP STAGE

This game was the first sign that Brazil, the
2014 tournament's host, was filled with anx-
iety playing in their home country. Mexico's
Ochoa made several great saves, including
a point-blank shot by Brazilian superstar
Neymar—Ochoa dove to his left to block
the shot with his body. Brazil's frustrations
grew, and the game ended in a 0–0 tie.

5. IKER CASILLAS, SPAIN VS. NETHERLANDS, 2010, FINAL

In a scoreless second half, Dutch winger Arjen Robben received a pass and came charging straight at Spain's Iker Casillas. Robben shot and Casillas casually knocked the direct bullet out of harm's way with his right leg. Robben dropped to his knees in disbelief. It would still take a long battle, but Spain would win the World Cup.

4. LEV YASHIN, SOVIET UNION VS. CHILE, 1962, QUARTERFINALS

For many years, the Soviet Union's Lev Yashin was considered the greatest goal-keeper in history. He was the only male keeper to win the Ballon d'Or. His save in the quarterfinals of the 1962 World Cup was the perfect display of his incredible talent. Chilean forward Honorino Landa was charging straight at him. Wearing all black, which earned him the nick-name "the Black Spider," Yashin stood his ground and dove low to his right to make the stop! Despite his heroics, Chile won the game 2–1.

3. TONI TUREK, WEST GERMANY VS. HUNGARY, 1952, FINAL

Hungary was the favorite to win the World Cup, considered one of the great teams of all time. Hungary destroyed teams, including host West Germany by the score of 8–3 in group play, on its way to the final. But in the final, a rematch, West German goalie Toni Turek was masterful. His best save may have come in the 24th minute when Nándor Hidegkuti had a clear shot at goal and Turek punched the ball over the top with his left hand. Germany won 3–2.

2. GIANLUIGI BUFFON, ITALY VS. FRANCE, 2006, FINAL

Italy was riding on the shoulders of Gianluigi Buffon in 2006. He had made remarkable saves throughout the tournament, including a legendary one against Lukas Podolski in the semifinal win over

Germany. In the final, with the score tied early at 1–1, Zinedine Zidane rose up and slammed the ball with his head. It looked like a classic Zidane header that would give France the lead, but Buffon leapt up and pushed the ball over the crossbar. That was just the beginning of a remarkable game: Zidane would be ejected in overtime and Buffon would be the hero in the penalty kick victory.

1. **GORDON BANKS**, ENGLAND VS. BRAZIL, 1970, GROUP STAGE

It wasn't in a final. But it involves Pelé, so this save has made its way into lore as the greatest of all time. Defending champions England were taking on the supremely talented Brazilians. Pelé rose in the air and headed the ball toward the ground and into the net. English goalkeeper Banks dove backward and low and punched the ball out. Pelé and the crowd were stunned, though Brazil would get one past Banks in the 59th minute and go on to win the World Cup.

▶ ▶ ▶ **EXTRA TIME**

WORLD CUP HIGHLIGHTS

The World Cup is the greatest sporting event on the planet. If you want to argue, you'll have to take it up with the millions—maybe billions—of fans who agree.

The event takes place every four years, heightening the anticipation. It showcases the sport that the world is most passionate about. The World Cup is almost always packed full of upsets and political intrigue. And it gets the entire planet involved.

The Olympics are special too—more countries are involved, more athletes are on hand for a large peaceable gathering, and the Games also are highly anticipated, coming in four-year cycles.

But the World Cup is different in that everyone is playing the same sport. *The* sport that is played around the world. The teams that have qualified have already fought their way through to get to the world's ultimate tournament.

There's no other event like it.

Even if you want to argue that there's a greater sporting event out there, one thing is certain: the World Cup is the most *popular* sporting event around. That's just a fact. In 2014 an estimated 3.2 billion tuned in to watch the World Cup, close to half the world's population. An estimated one billion watched the final between Germany and Argentina. Who knows how many will watch the 2018 World Cup in Russia, waiting for the latest chapter of soccer's global story?

While you're considering the future, why don't we take a trip back to the past. Here's a brief look at the history of the first twenty World Cups.

1. 1930, URUGUAY / WINNER: URUGUAY

The first World Cup was awarded in 1928, thanks to the success of the Olympic tournament in 1924, when organizers saw the enthusiasm for an international tournament. But the Olympics were open only to amateur players, while the greatest pro stars in the world had no choice but to watch at home as a winner was crowned the global champion. FIFA organizers had other ideas—they wanted to include soccer professionals to determine the true champion of the world.

Some countries, most notably England, objected to the professionalism in the World Cup and refused to participate in the original tournament.

Uruguay, a small country in South America with a rich soccer tradition, and the winner of the Olympic championship in 1924 (and again in 1928, a few days after the World Cup had already been awarded), was named as host. But the decision incensed European nations that had hoped to host the games, and many refused to go. Only four European nations—Belgium, France, Romania, and Yugoslavia—made the long voyage to South America.

The field of thirteen teams was heavily weighted toward South America, with seven teams from that continent, just four from Europe, plus the United States and Mexico. There was no qualifying tournament and with so few strong soccer nations involved, the United States had an easier path than it ever would again. The hodgepodge American team beat both Belgium and Paraguay by scores of 3–0. Against Paraguay, twenty-year-old American Bert Patenaude scored the first hat trick in World Cup history, though it took more than seventy years for that to be officially recognized.

The Americans lost 6–1 to Argentina in the

semifinal and finished third, the best-ever finish by an American team, though it is usually considered with an asterisk because 1930 was such an unusual tournament with so few participants.

In front of a crowd of 68,346 people, Uruguay beat Argentina 4–2 in the final, starting a tradition of the host country raising the championship trophy. In six of the twenty World Cups, the host nation has won.

2. 1934, ITALY / WINNER: ITALY

Like all of the early World Cups, little is known about the games of the second World Cup except from the reports of the media in attendance. In Italy, where fascist leader Benito Mussolini had risen to power, the local media was controlled by the state so there was even less transparency about how the event unfolded.

Mussolini understood the power of sports to both unify a country and spread propaganda. And he used the 1934 World Cup to advertise his fascist cultural beliefs to the world. The poster for the event featured a player with his arm outstretched in an apparent fascist salute. Everything about the event was officially described as glorious. However, during the World

Cup—even with the control of the media—there were many questions about the officiating and whether games were played fairly.

Uruguay, the defending champions, boycotted the event in retaliation for Italy and other European nations skipping the previous World Cup, making it the only nation in history not to try to defend its title. Meanwhile, England and its British neighbors remained in a dispute with FIFA over amateurism vs. professionalism.

Sixteen teams competed, with every game a knockout game—with so few teams, there was no need for a group stage like there is today. The only non-European teams were the United States, Egypt, Brazil, and Argentina. Italy knocked out the Americans immediately by a score of 7–1. For the second straight World Cup, the host country won. Italy defeated Czechoslovakia 2–1 in the final.

3. 1938, FRANCE / WINNER: ITALY

Politics continued to override sport in the third World Cup, the last one before the event was suspended because of World War II. Organizers decided to keep the tournament in Europe, despite the prospect of war on the horizon. Argentina had applied to host and, angry over being denied, did not participate. Yet again, neither did Uruguay. The only non-European teams were Brazil and Cuba; in fact, it was the first and only time Cuba ever competed in a World Cup (as of 2017). Disappointingly, the United States failed to qualify.

Austria was not a participant, as the country had been annexed by Hitler's Germany by that point. Spain did not participate, since it was engulfed in civil war. Though Adolf Hitler hoped to use the World Cup to show off Nazi Germany's dominance, Switzerland eliminated Germany.

The star of the tournament was the Brazilian team, which traveled to Europe for the first time. They dazzled the European fans. Leônidas da Silva, considered the father of Brazilian soccer, scored seven goals in the tournament. But Brazil was ousted by Italy in a semifinal game. Italy went on to defeat Hungary in the final. The Azzurri became the first nonhost to win the World Cup, and the first to win consecutive titles.

4. 1950, BRAZIL / WINNER: URUGUAY

The World Cup returned after a twelve-year hiatus

caused by World War II. In many ways this could be considered the first "true" World Cup since the post–World War II world was more accommodating to global travel now that an international war was not being waged.

Still, only thirteen teams participated. France withdrew because of a difficult travel schedule. Argentina, Scotland, Turkey, and India also declined to participate. Germany and Japan were banned from the tournament because of their roles in the war. England was involved for the first time and was considered one of the favorites, but it was eliminated in shocking fashion, losing 1–0 to a ragtag group of amateurs from the United States.

Brazil had built the world's largest stadium for the event, the Maracanã in Rio de Janeiro, and the country was prepared for a soccer coronation. Brazil was a heavy favorite to win the trophy, and a record crowd of 199,854 showed up for the final. Brazilians were so confident their team would win that a victory speech had already been prepared and, in preparation for the next day, newspapers had already printed headlines declaring a Brazilian win. But in the final, against Uruguay, Brazil was stunned. Uruguay won

2–1, breaking the hearts of the entire country, including a young boy named Pelé.

The defeat became known as the "Maracanazo," which translates as the "Maracanã blow," a fitting name since the loss was certainly a blow to the nation's self-esteem. The Brazilian team adopted yellow uniform shirts after the loss, to avoid the white ones they had worn that day.

Meanwhile, after four World Cups, Uruguay and Italy had each won a pair.

5. 1954, SWITZERLAND / WINNER: WEST GERMANY

Switzerland was named the host of the 1954 World Cup eight years before it was to be held, as much of the rest of Europe was recovering from the devastating consequences of war, while neutral Switzerland remained relatively unscathed. The tournament was the first to be televised. It was the highest-scoring World Cup in history, with 140 goals produced in twenty-six games.

Hungary entered the tournament as a world power. The Olympic champions in 1952, Hungary came into the tournament with twenty-three wins and four draws over the preceding four years, including a 6–3 devastation over England at Wembley, the first time a foreign team had won at that stadium. The star of the team was high-scoring forward Ferenc Puskás.

Hungary made it to the final in a rain-soaked stadium in the city of Bern. There it met West Germany (after World War II, Germany was temporarily divided into two countries), a team that had not been expected to do much in the World Cup and certainly not against Hungary, which had previously crushed the Germans 8–3 in the first round. Hungary took an early 2–0 lead eight minutes into the match, with Puskás scoring one of the goals. West Germany was on the brink of disaster. But by the 18th minute, West Germany, miraculously, had tied the game. After four goals were scored in eighteen minutes, the teams went scoreless for the next sixty-six minutes, until the 84th minute, when West German forward Helmut Rahn scored the game-winner, his second of the game, securing his distinguished place in soccer history.

The win lifted the spirits of the severely damaged postwar psyche of the Germans and is often considered a turning point for modern Germany. It also proved to be an inspiration for future generations of players, including a youngster named Franz Beckenbauer.

6. 1958, SWEDEN / WINNER: BRAZIL

Half a world away from his home, in a northernmost country far from his southern land, the greatest football player of all time was unveiled at the 1958 World Cup.

Seventeen-year-old Pelé made the World Cup in Sweden his personal stage and catapulted Brazil to the top of the world. He was paired with another phenomenal attacker, Garrincha, to create a beautiful, flowing form of soccer.

In the quarterfinals, Pelé started to steal the show, scoring the only goal to beat Wales 1–0. He scored a hat trick over a talented French team to put Brazil in the finals, where they would try to redeem their loss from eight years earlier.

Though Sweden took an early lead in the final, putting mental pressure on the Brazilians, Pelé and his teammates quickly overcame the deficit. Pelé scored two second-half goals in the eventual 5–2 rout. Brazil was finally the champion of the world, and just getting started on an amazing run of domination.

7. 1962, CHILE / WINNER: BRAZIL

Chile was awarded the 1962 World Cup, but two years before the event, the country suffered a devastating earthquake, causing severe damage and killing thousands. Despite that, the World Cup was held without many problems.

If Brazil hadn't staked its claim again as the greatest team in the world, the 1962 tournament might have been remembered for ugly, violent soccer games. One was called the Battle of Santiago, when Chile and Italy had a fight-filled game.

The World Cup was marred when Pelé went down with a pulled groin muscle in the second game. It was a huge blow to Brazil; Pelé was just twenty-one and expected to be even better than he had been four years earlier. But he was lost for the rest of the tournament.

Pelé's running mate Garrincha stepped into the spotlight and led Brazil to its second straight World Cup. Garrincha was one of nine returning members from the 1958 championship team.

Brazil beat Czechoslovakia 3–1 in the final, with one of the goals coming from Pelé's replacement, Amarildo.

Think about that for a second: a team lost its superstar, a legend, the greatest ever, and still won it all. That's how deep Brazil's lineup was.

8. 1966, ENGLAND / WINNER: ENGLAND

Sixteen years after England finally decided to play in the World Cup, the country hosted the event. And it became the third host to hoist the championship trophy.

The event was received enthusiastically by the soccer-mad public and set a record for the largest average attendance, which stood until 1994.

Brazil hoped to win an unprecedented third straight title. And the team was a heavy favorite. The team's composition was split between two generations: the original champions of 1950 and the newcomers. Plus, Brazil had Pelé, just twenty-five and in his prime.

But in Brazil's first game against Bulgaria, Pelé again suffered an injury. That game was the last time he and Garrincha would ever play together. Pelé had to sit out the next game against Hungary, which Brazil lost. He returned to play against Portugal but was subjected to vicious tackles as he was the focus of the defense. Brazil, shockingly, did not advance, and afterward a frustrated Pelé said he would never play in another World Cup.

On its way to a hometown final, England defeated Argentina and Portugal. Team star and captain Bobby Charlton scored both goals in the semifinal win that put England in the final against West Germany. In that thrilling game, English forward Geoff Hurst scored a hat trick, which included one of the most controversial goals in history, the one that put England ahead for good in extra time. The ball bounced off the crossbar and into the goal, though there was a debate about whether it crossed the line.

Hurst scored an insurance goal in the 120th minute, though it didn't end the debate, which—like all good World Cup controversies—raged on for decades.

9. 1970, MEXICO / WINNER: BRAZIL

By 1970, most of the world had TVs, the globe felt smaller thanks to an increase in international travel, and everyone on the planet knew about Pelé. In that way, the 1970 World Cup might have been the first truly global tournament.

The event matched some of the most passionate soccer fans in the world, in Mexico, with the most beautiful soccer team: Brazil. It made for a colorful, exciting tournament that convinced millions that World Cup soccer was a unique, must-see sporting event. But the new television audience created concerns: there were heat and altitude issues in Mexico, but because of the time difference, the games were played at midday to satisfy the European television audience.

Pelé, frustrated by constant fouling and a lack of protection by the referees, had said he wouldn't return to the World Cup. But he did, at age twenty-nine, for one last shot at glory.

A young Franz Beckenbauer was also in the tournament, playing alongside the great German Gerd Müller. Both men would challenge Pelé for the title of best in the world.

Brazil cruised through group play, including a 1–0 win over defending champion England. In the semifinals, the Brazilians exorcised the ghosts from 1950, with a 3–1 defeat over Uruguay. In the other semifinal, Italy beat Germany; Beckenbauer played the game in a sling after his shoulder was dislocated.

In a meeting of the only two countries to win

consecutive World Cups, Brazil dominated Italy 4–1. It was Brazil's third title in four attempts, an unparalleled run of dominance.

Pelé, in what would truly be his final World Cup performance, scored in the 18th minute of the game. In the course of his World Cup career, he took the tournament from an interesting sporting event to a global phenomenon.

10. 1974, WEST GERMANY / WINNER: WEST GERMANY

The Germans hosted the 1974 World Cup. The Germans won the 1974 World Cup. But that World Cup is most often remembered for the man whose team finished second, Johan Cruyff of the Netherlands.

Cruyff stepped into the void vacated by Pelé and was anointed the best player on the globe. The Dutch hadn't been in a World Cup since 1934, but that didn't preclude them from becoming one of the favorites. They played a style called Total Football, coached by Rinus Michels, who later took his system to Barcelona and launched a new generation of soccer stars.

The style was so distinct and masterful that Carlos

Alberto, captain of the 1970 Brazilian World Cup championship team, once said, "The only team I've seen that did things differently was Holland at the 1974 World Cup in Germany. Since then everything looks more or less the same to me . . . Their 'carousel' style of play was amazing to watch and marvelous for the game."

There was concern about the host country, as two years earlier there had been a terrorist attack at the Munich Olympics by Palestinian terrorists. That caused heightened tensions, as did the qualification of East Germany. The emotional match between the divided German teams was heavily secured by police: East Germany shocked the more dominant West German team with a 1–0 win.

The World Cup was marked by modern concerns. There were pay disputes on some teams. Sponsorship deals started to get in the way—Cruyff refused to wear the Adidas uniform because he had a deal with Puma, so the Netherlands federation created a special two-stripe jersey for him.

The Netherlands, the new kids on the block, cruised through the tournament, a triumphant statement from a debut squad. But when the team met West Germany in the final, the German defense shut down

Cruyff and won the game 2–1, the fourth time the host country had won the championship.

Yet to this day, the legend of Cruyff lives on.

11. 1978, ARGENTINA / WINNER: ARGENTINA

As in past World Cups, politics played a huge part in the 1978 World Cup. Host Argentina had experienced a military coup two years before the tournament, long after the bid had been awarded. The country was ripped apart; citizens disappeared, thousands had been arrested, and there were high-profile assassinations and human rights violations.

But the tournament went on as planned. Though there were charges of corruption on the playing field as well, the competition was compelling.

The once and future stars of soccer were both missing. Johan Cruyff abruptly retired from international competition before the World Cup. Some thought it was due to his strong feelings about the political situation; three decades later it came out that Cruyff's family had received kidnap threats and he feared for their safety if he was gone. Argentina's coach controversially left soccer's future star Diego

Maradona off the squad, saying the seventeen-year-old was too young.

Despite those absences, the Netherlands and Argentina met in the final, the first time in twenty years that the final hosted two teams who had never won the championship.

Again, the host hoisted the trophy: Argentina defeated the Dutch 3–1.

12. 1982, SPAIN / WINNER: ITALY

The 1982 World Cup was one of inclusion: the tournament expanded from sixteen to twenty-four teams in an effort to open the party to more countries. For the first time, Algeria, Cameroon, New Zealand, Honduras, and Kuwait participated. However, a few notable teams had failed to qualify, including the Netherlands, Mexico, and Sweden. Though Diego Maradona made his World Cup debut, defending champ Argentina was knocked out in the second round-robin group play.

In the two-group-stage format, no one would have expected who the ultimate champion was. While England and Brazil looked like the dominant teams, Italy didn't win a game in group play with three draws.

But the lesson of 1982 was to just advance and see what happened.

In the final, the two stalwarts, Italy—who advanced despite their lukewarm play in the group stage—and West Germany met. West Germany had advanced by beating the talented French—led by Michel Platini—on penalty kicks. Italy's star was Paolo Rossi, who scored in the 3-1 championship win with his sixth goal of the tournament.

13. 1986, MEXICO / WINNER: ARGENTINA

The stage for the 1986 World Cup was Mexico, but the star was an Argentinian by the name of Maradona, who dominated the tournament from start to finish.

The competition was originally supposed to be held in Colombia, but that country had financial problems so the tournament—with just three years' notice—went back to Mexico sixteen years after it had first hosted. Mexico was able to pull off the event, despite suffering a massive earthquake just eight months before the opener.

Maradona's talent was the story of the tournament. In the quarterfinal match against England—the first time the countries had played soccer since engaging in the Falkland Wars in 1982—Maradona wrote history.

First he scored the controversial Hand of God goal, arriving in the box at the same time as the goalkeeper and knocking the ball into the net with his left hand. England protested but the official let the goal stand and Maradona later gave it the famous title. A few minutes later Maradona scored what was dubbed the Goal of the Century with a nine-touch journey to the goal that included a 180-degree turn and left the entire England side helplessly watching.

Maradona again scored two goals in the 2–0 defeat over Belgium in the semifinals. Though he didn't score in the final victory over West Germany, his presence changed the dynamic of the game. Argentina won 3–2 and there was a new "best player in the world."

14. 1990, ITALY / WINNER: WEST GERMANY

The reviews for the 1990 World Cup were almost universally poor: the tournament featured defensive soccer, with coaches trying not to lose rather than attacking to win. It was the lowest-scoring World Cup in history.

That wasn't good news for American organizers, who would host the next World Cup and were hoping for some dazzling displays that might convince the American public that soccer was thrilling. But the good news was that despite the poor play, at the time, it was the most-watched World Cup in history, though the record has since been broken. More good news: the United States finally, for the first time since 1950, qualified for the World Cup.

The Americans' stay didn't last long. They were dominated in their opener, 5–1, by Czechoslovakia and lost their other two games. Teams that were usually open and attacking, like Brazil and Argentina, also played a defensive style. The defending champion Argentina lost their opener to Cameroon.

Host Italy was eliminated by Argentina in the semifinals, setting up a rematch of the 1986 final. West Germany—the last time it would play as a separate country before reunification—got revenge, winning 1–0. Fitting for the tournament, the only goal came on a penalty kick. Franz Beckenbauer, who had won the World Cup as a player, won it again as the West German coach.

15. 1994, UNITED STATES / WINNER: BRAZIL

When the United States was chosen to host its first World Cup, most of the soccer world was appalled. At the time of the selection, in 1988, the U.S. men's team had never qualified for a modern World Cup (it would in 1990). Though everyone else referred to the sport as *football*, Americans called the world's game *soccer* and thought it was something played by little kids. They knew about Pelé, because he had played for the New York Cosmos, but that was about all their knowledge: most people barely even knew the rules.

But FIFA saw an enormous, untapped market and a way to spread the game beyond the strongholds of Europe and South America. Plus, the United States had huge stadiums and knew how to promote sports. Part of the agreement was that a professional league would be launched in the United States following the tournament, which was how Major League Soccer was later born.

It was the last World Cup with twenty-four teams, before expanding to thirty-two. The games were held in nine cities and, given the size of the United States, there were concerns about the long distances some teams would have to travel between games.

All of the stadiums had a capacity of at least 57,000 and the attendance for the tournament was almost 3.6 million, a record that still stands.

The United States automatically qualified as hosts and provided early surprises. The Americans tied Switzerland in the opening game. The second game provided shock and also tragedy. Colombia defender Andrés Escobar put the ball into the back of his own net for an own goal that gave the U.S. team a 1–0 lead and led to the eventual win and a berth in the second round. It was the Americans' first World Cup victory since 1950. But devastatingly, Escobar was murdered when he went home to Colombia, reportedly because of his mistake on the soccer field.

The Americans moved into the knockout round and played Brazil on the Fourth of July at Stanford. It was a defensive, ugly battle. American midfielder Tab Ramos took an elbow to the head from Brazilian Leonardo, which fractured his skull. Leonardo was sent off, but even though the U.S. team had a man advantage for the entire second half, Brazil won 1–0.

The tournament also marked the end of Diego

Maradona's career. He was sent home in shame after failing a drug test. Saudi Arabia was a surprise team, making it to the second round. In another shocker, Bulgaria made it to the semifinals by knocking off Germany.

The final was exactly the kind of game the American promoters dreaded, as Italy and Brazil ended ninety minutes of regulation and thirty minutes of extra time in a scoreless tie and went to penalty kicks, the first time the World Cup had ever been decided on penalties. Brazil won 3–2, with Italian star Roberto Baggio sailing his attempt to tie the score over the crossbar. It was the fourth title for Brazil.

16. 1998, FRANCE / WINNER: FRANCE

The World Cup expanded again in 1998, this time to thirty-two teams in another effort to include more countries. Despite the change, a prevailing theme of the World Cup continued: the host won. However, France may have been the most unlikely host to lift the trophy.

Brazil came into the tournament as the heavy favorite to repeat. The talented side had added

Ronaldo, considered the greatest player in the world. But it wasn't all a dance of the samba to the final for Brazil, which lost to Norway in group play.

Among the intriguing matches in 1998 was another emotional battle between Argentina and England, twelve years after the Hand of God. In the match in Saint-Étienne, young English star David Beckham was sent off for kicking an Argentinian player. Argentina prevailed on penalty kicks. Iran played the United States, a game expected to be marked by the hostility between the nations at the time. The Iranian ayatollah had even forbidden his nation's team from walking toward the Americans as part of the ceremonial prematch handshake. But despite expectations, Iranians in the stands used the event to protest their government, and their team prevailed. The Americans again had an unsuccessful stay in the World Cup, losing all three games and finishing last of the thirty-two teams.

The French team captured the imagination of its country, with its multiethnic makeup. France gained momentum as it progressed through the tournament, led by talented midfielder Zinedine Zidane, who was of North African descent. Still, when France reached the finals, Les Bleus were a huge underdog to Brazil.

But the day of the final, Ronaldo had a seizure and was originally scratched from the lineup. Then, shortly before the game, he was reinserted into Brazil's starting eleven. The strange incident caused mass confusion and conspiracy theories. Ronaldo played but was a shadow of the player who had been dominating up until that point. Instead the star of the show was Zidane, who headed in two goals and led France to a shocking 3–0 victory. Afterward, over a million fans flooded the streets of Paris to celebrate.

17. 2002, JAPAN–SOUTH KOREA / WINNER: BRAZIL

The first World Cup to be held in Asia was also the only World Cup to be co-hosted in a joint bid. The location created a new problem for soccer fans around the world because—for many fans in Europe and South America—games were held in the middle of the night or early morning because of the time difference.

The tournament held several surprises and upsets, including the fate of both hosts. Japan advanced to the second round for the first time, and South Korea made it all the way to the semifinals before losing to Germany. Senegal and Turkey exceeded expectations and met in a quarterfinal. The Americans were also a surprising story: the team led by young star Landon Donovan advanced to the quarterfinals for the first time in modern history, beating Mexico in the knockout round, before losing to Germany 1–0.

Among the surprising losers: defending champions France and perennial power Argentina both were eliminated in group play.

But in the end, it was two World Cup superpowers in the final. Brazil beat Germany 2–0, culminating a redemption tour by Ronaldo, who had fought off the demons of the 1998 tournament to become a world champion. It was an unprecedented fifth championship for Brazil.

18. 2006, GERMANY / WINNER: ITALY

Head butt. Say those two words to any soccer fan and they will know what World Cup you are referencing. The 2006 tournament in Germany.

Germany hosted its first World Cup since its reunification, and the tournament was a roaring success. An efficient train system carried fans quickly between games, large gatherings known as "fan miles" in public parks—with enormous screens—created a festive atmosphere, and the soccer was high quality. Germany's team, coached by former player Jürgen Klinsmann, was exciting, and many Germans reported feeling a national pride for the first time since the country had reunified.

Though there were upsets—including the advancements of Australia, Ecuador, and Ukraine—many of the traditional powers advanced, piquing interest and setting up intriguing knockout games, like Argentina vs. Mexico, Spain vs. France, and Portugal vs. England.

Host Germany was ousted in a semifinal by Italy, and France got past Portugal—a team led by a talented young Cristiano Ronaldo. Italy and France met in the final, and France was expected to have the upper hand. France got off to an early lead, on a goal from Zinedine Zidane. But Italy equalized on a shot from Marco Materazzi, and then the game became a defensive battle, one that headed into extra time.

Near the end of extra time, Zidane turned around and head-butted Materazzi in the chest, in response to insults from the Italian player. Zidane was sent off but no more goals were scored and the game went to penalty kicks. Italy prevailed and pulled off the upset.

The Italians won the trophy, but the enduring image from the tournament is of Zidane's head butt.

19. 2010, SOUTH AFRICA / WINNER: SPAIN

For years, the world had been waiting for the talented Spanish football team to produce at a World Cup. In South Africa, the wait was over. The team that had won the 2008 European Championship finally broke through in the world's biggest tournament.

The World Cup ventured to a new continent again in 2010: Africa. There were concerns about whether stadiums would be ready as well as about high crime rates in South Africa, but the event went smoothly. It did not, however, provide a big boost to African nations. Only Ghana advanced to the knockout round, where they eliminated the United States, which had gotten through group play on a thrilling added-time goal by Landon Donovan in the final group game against Algeria.

Germany made it to the semifinals, where the team flashed the brilliance it would exhibit four years later. Uruguay showed that it was not just a team with a World Cup past, but a present, also making it to the semifinals.

The final matchup between the Netherlands and Spain was one embraced by soccer historians: two teams with a joined past in terms of style of play, a kind of blood brothers. Seven of Spain's starting eleven played for Barcelona, the club that had perfected the tiki-taka philosophy that had originated in the Netherlands with Johan Cruyff.

But in truth, the final was not a beautiful game. The Dutch relied more on physically disrupting their opponents. Fourteen yellow cards were issued, nine for the Netherlands and five for Spain. One Dutch player was sent off for a hard foul, and another likely should have been for an aggressive kick to the chest of a Spaniard. Finally, in the 116th minute, Spain's brilliant midfielder Andrés Iniesta scored the only goal of the match, and Spain became the eighth nation to win a World Cup.

20. 2014, BRAZIL / WINNER: GERMANY

The World Cup returned to Brazil for the first time since the great humbling at Maracanã. Many in the nation of devoted football fans were excited but wary: Brazil had been named the host in 2007, when the country's economy was strong. But by 2014, when the World Cup was held, the economy had weakened significantly and there were concerns about the country's readiness and ability to host such a massive event. Protesters took to the streets. That was a foreshadowing of what would occur two years later with the Rio Olympics.

Every team that had won a past World Cup qualified for the tournament. But defending champions Spain and 2006 champions Italy were both eliminated in group play. The U.S. team, coached by German legend Jürgen Klinsmann, made it through group play thanks to a win over Ghana and a draw with Portugal. But then the Americans were ousted by Belgium, one of the favorites.

Brazil's hopes of avenging the 1950 disappointment were stopped abruptly in the semifinals, where the team was humiliated by Germany, 7–1. It was the worst defeat in Brazil's long World Cup history and became etched on the nation's soul, the way the defeat sixty-four years earlier had been: the score became slang for anything horribly humiliating.

Lionel Messi's Argentina advanced to the final on the other side of the draw, though Messi—who had scored four goals in group play—didn't score in the knockout rounds. During the beginning of the final match, it appeared that Germany might have used up all its goals in the semifinal, but finally, in the 113th minute of extra time, twenty-two-year-old substitute Mario Götze pushed in the winning goal.

Germany won the World Cup for the fourth time, and the European continent held on to the championship trophy for the third straight cycle.

UPCOMING WORLD CUPS

2018 WORLD CUP
Host: Russia

Venues in eleven cities: Kaliningrad, Kazan, Moscow, Nizhny Novgorod, Rostov-on-Don, Saint Petersburg, Samara, Saransk, Sochi, Volgograd, and Yekaterinburg

Dates: June 14 to July 15, 2018

2022 WORLD CUP
Host: Qatar

Dates: November 21 to December 18, 2022

TOP TEN
(OR TOP ELEVEN WITH TIES!)
HIGHEST GOAL SCORERS
IN INTERNATIONAL HISTORY

8. **(TIE) KINNAH PHIRI**, MALAWI: 71 GOALS IN 115 MATCHES; **KIATISUK SENAMUANG**, THAILAND: 71 GOALS IN 134 MATCHES; **MIROSLAV KLOSE**, GERMANY: 71 GOALS IN 137 MATCHES

7. **BASHAR ABDULLAH**, KUWAIT: 75 GOALS IN 143 MATCHES

6. **PELÉ**, BRAZIL: 77 GOALS IN 92 MATCHES

5. **HUSSEIN SAEED**, IRAQ: 78 GOALS IN 137 MATCHES

4. **(TIE) GODFREY CHITALU**, ZAMBIA: 79 GOALS IN 111 CAPS; **CRISTIANO RONALDO**, PORTUGAL: 79 GOALS IN 147 MATCHES

3. **KUNISHIGE KAMAMOTO**, JAPAN: 80 GOALS IN 84 CAPS

2. **FERENC PUSKÁS**, HUNGARY: 84 GOALS IN 85 CAPS

1. **ALI DAEI**, IRAN: 109 INTERNATIONAL GOALS IN 149 CAPS

▶ ▶ ▶ PENALTY KICKS

THE NEXT GENERATION OF SUPERSTARS

TIM WEAH, UNITED STATES

. . . .

Background: Weah is a familiar name to many soccer fans. Tim's father, George, is considered one of the greatest players to ever come from the African continent. The Liberian forward was the 1995 FIFA World Player of the Year, and won the Ballon d'Or the same year (before the awards were combined). A year later he finished second to Ronaldo. He had a successful career for Paris Saint-Germain, Monaco, and AC Milan but was never able to help his own country become a power. His son was born in Brooklyn in 2000 and grew up in both New York and Florida. Tim played for his uncle Michael's soccer club in Queens and eventually with the Red Bull Development Academy team. He was spotted by his father's old club, PSG, and joined the club's academy. By 2017 he had signed a professional contract and was playing with PSG's U-19 team, as well as in the U.S. Youth national program.

Skill Set: An aggressive attacker, either on the wing or as a center forward. With next-level speed and an eye for the goal, Tim appears to play with both the fearlessness and joy that were trademarks of his father.

Breakout Moment: In October of 2017, Weah scored a hat trick against Paraguay at the U-17 World Cup to put the Americans into the quarterfinals against England. The performance came just days after the senior team had been eliminated from World Cup contention, and made dejected American fans optimistic that the future could be brighter.

PAUL ARRIOLA, UNITED STATES

. . . .

Background: Arriola grew up in Southern California and played for the U.S. Soccer Development Academy based in Temecula. When he was seventeen, he signed with Club Tijuana of the Liga MX, a team he had trained with earlier. He played there for four years before joining MLS in 2017. The Los Angeles Galaxy held his rights but traded them to D.C. United for a transfer fee reportedly in excess of $3 million, an impressive price tag. Arriola played in U.S. Soccer's youth system, including the Under-17 World Cup in 2011. He made his senior debut with the national team in 2016 and became a trusted regular under Bruce Arena.

Skill Set: Another attacking midfielder who plays on the wing, Arriola has speed, vision, and good ball control. He is a tenacious defender.

Breakout Moment: Arriola scored a goal in each of his first two appearances with the national team in 2016, against Puerto Rico and Trinidad and Tobago.

CAMERON CARTER-VICKERS, UNITED STATES

Background: Carter-Vickers, born in 1997, grew up in England. However, his father is a retired American basketball player, so he plays for the U.S. national team. When he was eleven, he joined the academy system of Premier League club Tottenham Hotspur. He made his first team debut in 2016 and his first start in January 2017. On the international front, Carter-Vickers represented the United States at the Under-20 World Cup in 2015. A year later he made his debut with the U.S. senior team.

Skill Set: A large, physical center back, Carter-Vickers is very strong, a key defender, and a hard worker.

Breakout Moment: Carter-Vickers jumped onto the radar for future prospects when he was named Man

of the Match in a 1–0 defeat of Senegal in the Under-20
World Cup in 2017.

ETHAN HORVATH, UNITED STATES

Background: Considered the American goalkeeper
of the future, Horvath was born in 1995 in Colorado.
He grew up playing in the U.S. Soccer Development
Academy. When he was seventeen, he signed his first
professional contract with Molde FK in Norway. He
played there for four seasons, becoming the starting
goalkeeper when he was just twenty. In 2017, he signed
with the Dutch side, Club Brugge. He rose through U.S.
Soccer youth levels and was the starting goalkeeper on
the U-23 team that lost an Olympic qualifying game.

Skill Set: Tall and lanky, Horvath is strong at keeping
his defense organized.

Breakout Moment: In 2016, he made his U.S. national
team debut, with a clean sheet in the 2–0 win over Cuba.

KYLIAN MBAPPÉ, FRANCE

Background: Considered the top prospect in the
world, Mbappé was born in a suburb of Paris just

months after France won its first World Cup. Now he is considered the future of the team. Originally coached by his father on his youth club, AS Bondy, he went to the French training academy at Clairefontaine. Many European clubs tried to sign him, but he finally landed at AS Monaco. He debuted with the first team in December 2016, still just sixteen years old. He led France to a U-19 European championship. He made his debut with the French senior team in March 2017. Later that year, a bidding war erupted for his services between Paris Saint-Germain (PSG) and Real Madrid; Mbappé landed with PSG for an extraordinary sum of roughly $175 million.

Skill Set: Possesses speed, smarts, quick decision-making ability, quick reactions, and an impressive goal-scoring ability.

Breakout Moment: In February 2016, Mbappé scored a stoppage time goal for Monaco, becoming the youngest to do so in the club's history.

OUSMANE DEMBELE, FRANCE
. . . .

Background: If you were to pick a favorite for the 2022 World Cup based on prospects, your money would probably be on France. France has several of the top-rated young players in the world. In addition to Mbappé, Dembele, a forward, is another one. He was born in 1997 in northern France. He started playing at a young age and signed a contract with French club Rennes in 2014. In 2015 he made his debut with Rennes's first team. In 2016 he signed a contract with Borussia Dortmund, where he earned the Bundesliga Rookie of the Season award. In 2017, he was transferred to Barcelona.

He was first called up to the French national team in 2016.

Skill Set: An attacking, talented forward; excellent dribbler; good on the counterattack; and a threat on set pieces. Skilled with both feet.

Breakout Moment: In June 2017, Ousmane scored his first goal for the French team against England.

MARCO ASENSIO, SPAIN

Background: Born in Palma, Majorca, an island off Spain, Asensio joined the club RCD Mallorca when he was ten. In 2013, when he was seventeen, he made his debut with the senior team. A year later, Real Madrid signed him; he was lent back to Mallorca and then to Espanyol. He made his first start for Real Madrid in September 2016. Asensio grew up playing on Spanish youth teams and led Spain's U-15 to victory at the European Championship. He made his debut with the senior team in a friendly in May 2016. Asensio's mother was Dutch; she died of cancer when he was fifteen and Asensio dedicates his play to her.

Skill Set: The attacking midfielder is a creative play-maker, with excellent vision, decision-making, and passing skills.

Breakout Moment: Just twenty-one, Asensio came off the bench to score a goal against Juventus in the Champions League final.

MARCUS RASHFORD, ENGLAND

Background: Born in Manchester, England, Marcus seemed destined for greatness at an early age. He joined the academy system at Manchester United when he was seven. In 2015, shortly after he turned eighteen, he made the first team. The forward scored eight goals in his first season. Based on that performance he was called into England's European Championship squad in 2016 and started a friendly against Australia. He became the youngest player to ever represent England in the Euros.

Skill Set: Fast and fearless, the center forward is an excellent finisher.

Breakout Moment: In his Premier League debut against Arsenal he scored two goals and had an assist.

VINÍCIUS JÚNIOR, BRAZIL
. . . .

Background: Born in Rio de Janeiro in 2000, Vinícius José Paixão de Oliveira Júnior was only sixteen when he was tagged with the title "the next Neymar," a reference to the star of the Brazilian national team. Júnior was called into Brazil's under-15 team when he was thirteen. He attended a school affiliated with Brazilian club Flamengo beginning at age five, and his soccer skill always stood out. He made his debut with Flamengo in 2017. Real Madrid quickly signed a contract to acquire his rights when he was eighteen. He helped Brazil win the U-17 South American championship in March 2017.

Skill Set: Has a nose for the goal, and he's a strong dribbler, who is technically skilled.

Breakout Moment: At the Copa São Paulo, Júnior dominated the competition at sixteen even though he was playing against players three years older.

HIRVING LOZANO, MEXICO

. . . .

Background: Born in Mexico City in 1995, Lozano joined Pachuca's youth team when he was fourteen. He is nicknamed "Chucky" after a famous horror movie character, since Lozano, like the movie character, liked to hide under beds trying to scare his teammates when he was younger. He made his Liga MX debut when he was eighteen, against Club América, coming off the bench and scoring the only goal of the win at Azteca. He won the Golden Boot as the top scorer in the CONCACAF Champions League when he was twenty-one. Later that year, Dutch team PSV Eindhoven signed him to a six-year contract. He made his league debut in August and received a standing ovation from the home fans. Lozano played on the Mexican U-20 and U-23 teams and made his debut with the senior team in 2016, when he was twenty. He scored a goal for Mexico in the Confederations Cup in 2017.

Skill Set: Has a powerful right foot and is quick with or without the ball.

Breakout Moment: At the 2015 CONCACAF U-20 championships, he won the Golden Boot, scoring five goals.

GIANLUIGI DONNARUMMA, ITALY

. . . .

Background: Considered the world's next great goalkeeper, Donnarumma was born in Naples in 1999. He played for Napoli as a youngster but at fourteen was signed by AC Milan, where his older brother plays. He received a call-up to the senior team three days before his sixteenth birthday, but didn't play. He made his debut for the Milan senior team in October 2015. He made his debut with the Italian senior squad in August 2016.

Skill Set: Tall, rangy, and physical, Donnarumma has quick reactions and is a calm, commanding presence on defense.

Breakout Moment: Long considered Italy's top goalkeeping prospect, he made his first start against the Netherlands in 2017 in a 2–1 win.

TOP TEN BIGGEST UPSETS IN WORLD CUP HISTORY

One of the best things about soccer is that because it is such a low-scoring game, upsets occur frequently. The ball bounces a funny way, a team underestimates its opponent, and suddenly the unthinkable happens.

10. **COSTA RICA 1, ITALY 0**, 2014 GROUP STAGE

    Italy was a star-studded team, but Costa Rica beat the Italians on a goal just before half-time by Bryan Ruiz. The victory was part of the Ticos' remarkable run: they won their heavyweight group, which included England and Uruguay and made it all the way to the quarterfinals for the first time in their history. Italy was eliminated in group play.

9. **EAST GERMANY 1, WEST GERMANY 0**, 1974 GROUP STAGE

    In a game tense with political and emotional subplots, the team from the other side of the (Berlin) wall beat the hosts 1–0—the only time the divided country met in a World Cup. East German Jürgen Sparwasser scored in the 77th minute. West Germany was devastated, but the loss shocked them into action, and they went on to win the championship.

8. **WEST GERMANY 3, HUNGARY 2**, 1954 FINAL

The game was called the Miracle of Bern, a nod to the city where it was played, and the win took place long before West Germany was a world power. The Hungarians had been destroying the opposition for years and seemed unstoppable on the way to the final, including beating West Germany 8–3. The score was 2–2 at halftime, but in the 84th minute West German forward Helmut Rahn scored. Though Hungary thought it had the equalizer four minutes later, the goal was ruled offside.

7. **CAMEROON 1, ARGENTINA 0**, 1990 GROUP STAGE

In the first game of the 1990 World Cup, Cameroon shocked the world by upsetting the reigning champions. Cameroon shut down Diego Maradona and had two players sent off as a result of the physical play. Cameroon would reach the quarterfinals, the farthest an African team had gone in the World Cup.

6. **NORTH KOREA 1, ITALY 0**, 1966 GROUP STAGE
Italy was heavily favored over the little-known North Korean side, which was the first Asian nation to ever qualify for a World Cup. The hardworking underdogs became a favorite of the English crowd. The 1–0 upset was thanks to a goal from Pak Doo-ik. North Korea won its group and Italy was eliminated. The team would eventually squander a 3–0 lead in a 5–3 loss to Portugal.

5. **SENEGAL 1, FRANCE 0**, 2002 GROUP STAGE
France was the reigning champion of both the World Cup and the European Championship. Senegal was a huge underdog. The winning goal came in the 30th minute when Papa Bouda Diop buried a

rebound. The shocking upset was a sign of things to come for France—the team was eliminated without winning a game or scoring a goal. Senegal advanced to the quarterfinals.

4. **FRANCE 3, BRAZIL 0**, 1998 FINAL

Brazil was the defending champion and a heavy favorite. Host France had made a surprising run to the final and wasn't expected to do more. The morning of the game, Brazilian star Ronaldo had a seizure and was scratched from the lineup. He was reinserted shortly before the game but played with an odd lethargy. Zinedine Zidane scored two goals, heading in a pair of corner kicks. Emmanuel Petit added a late third goal to set off celebrations around Paris.

3. **USA 2, COLOMBIA 1**, 1994 GROUP STAGE

Colombia was one of the favorites in 1994. The Americans played tenacious defense and were helped by an early own goal from Colombian Andrés Escobar. Escobar was later shot and killed at home, believed to be targeted because of his mistake. The U.S. team added a second goal—Earnie Stewart scored on an assist by Tab Ramos—in the 52nd minute. Though Colombia got a late goal, the shocking upset eliminated the team. The U.S. team would lose to Brazil in the round of 16.

2. **URUGUAY 2, BRAZIL 1,** 1950 FINAL

Brazil already had the celebration planned for its sure victory at Maracanã Stadium. No one thought Brazil could be stopped, since it had won its previous two matches by a combined score of 13–2. Brazil had the country behind it and nearly 200,000 fans in the stands ready to celebrate. But Uruguay broke a 1–1 tie in the 79th minute with a goal from Alcides Ghiggia. The stadium went absolutely silent. The loss became known as *"El Maracanazo,"* "the Maracanã Blow"—it stunned the country and sent it into mourning.

1. USA 1, ENGLAND 0, 1950 GROUP STAGE

England was a professional soccer power-house. The Americans were a ragtag group of working-class semipros. The game at Belo Horizonte, Brazil, was expected to be a lopsided affair: the American coach even likened his team to "sheep ready to be slaughtered." But the American defense absorbed the unrelenting attack from England. The 1–0 win came thanks to Joe Gaetjens's goal in the 37th minute. The score was so unbelievable that many newspapers around the world assumed it was a mistake and reversed it in print. The Americans would not qualify for another World Cup for forty years.

CHAMPIONS
OF
MEN'S
SOCCER

Pelé (center) hugs his teammates after Brazil wins the 1970 World Cup Championship.
(Zuma/isiphotos.com)

Diego Maradona raises his hands in victory following Argentina's 1986 World Cup final win.
(Zuma/isiphotos.com)

Xavi (Spain) (left) jumps over the tackle of Mohammed Ameen (Saudi Arabia) (center) in a 2006 World Cup match. (Brad Smith/isiphotos.com)

Zinedine Zidane (left) of France fights aggressively for the ball against Gennaro Gattuso (right) of Italy in the 2006 World Cup final. (Brad Smith/isiphotos.com)

Brazilian Ronaldo (right) celebrates his goal with teammates Adriano (left) and Kaká (center) in a 2006 World Cup match against Ghana. (Brad Smith/isiphotos.com)

Italian goalkeeper Gianluigi Buffon (center) moves out of his goal to intercept a pass in a 2006 World Cup match against the USA. (Tony Quinn/isiphotos.com)

Landon Donovan (USA) heads the ball in a 2011 CONCACAF Gold Cup soccer match against Panama. (John Dorton/isiphotos.com)

Clint Dempsey (USA) (left) attempts a bicycle kick against Colombia in the 2016 Copa America Centenario. (John Todd/isiphotos.com)

Michael Bradley (USA) takes a corner kick in a 2018 World Cup qualifying match against Guatemala. (John Todd/isiphotos.com)

Jozy Altidore (USA) (center) launches the ball forward on a header in a 2018 World Cup qualifying match against Mexico. (John Dorton/isiphotos.com)

INDEX

1930 World Cup, 218–20
1934 World Cup, 220–21
1938 World Cup, 221–22
1950 World Cup, 139–40, 141–44, 222–24, 267, 268
1952 World Cup, 213
1954 World Cup, 45, 224–25, 264
1958 World Cup, 13, 99, 226
1962 World Cup, 15, 212, 227–28
1964 European Championship, 54
1966 World Cup, 15, 46, 97, 228–29, 265
1970 World Cup, 16, 46, 98–99, 214, 229–31
1974 World Cup, 47, 61, 98, 231–33, 263–64
1978 World Cup, 29, 61, 233–34
1982 World Cup, 30–31, 96, 210, 234–35
1986 World Cup, 31–32, 99–100, 235–36
1990 World Cup, 32–33, 49, 82, 156–57, 196–98, 236–37, 264–65, 1990
1994 World Cup, 82–83, 157–58, 199–200, 238–40, 266–67
1998 World Cup, 67–68, 76–77, 83, 91, 97–98, 150, 159–60, 189–90, 240–42, 266
2000 European Championship, 68, 83, 91
2002 World Cup, 68–69, 78, 83, 91, 122–23, 150, 190–91, 211, 242–43, 265–66
2004 European Championship, 91
2006 World Cup, 23, 39–40, 49, 69–70, 78, 91–92, 124, 151, 165, 213–14
2008 European Championship, 51–52, 54
2008 Olympics, 23–24, 181
2009 Confederations Cup, 135, 166
2010 European Championship, 55
2010 World Cup, 25, 40, 51–52, 55, 92, 94, 95–96, 124–26, 135–36, 166–67, 174, 211–12, 245–46
2012 European Championship, 51–52, 92
2014 World Cup, 25, 40, 92, 95, 126–27, 136–37, 167, 175–76, 183 84, 209–10, 211, 246–48, 263
2016 Copa América, 26
2016 European Championship, 40–41, 92
2017 Gold Cup, 177, 184–85
2018 World Cup, 26, 92, 176–77, 200, 248
2022 World Cup, 56, 248

A

Abdullah, Bashar, 249
AC Milan, 84, 85–86
addiction, 33
Adu, Freddy, 165, 179

Ajax, 59–60, 63
Alberto, Carlos, 98–99, 232
Al Sadd, 56
Altidore, Jozy
  2008 Olympics, 181
  2010 World Cup, 94, 125, 182
  2014 World Cup, 167, 183–84
  2017 Gold Cup, 184–85
  AZ, 182
  charitable activities, 185
  and Clint Dempsey, 184
  first American to score in La Liga, 181
  inconsistent performance, 182–84
  New York/New Jersey MetroStars, 180
  New York Red Bulls, 180–81
  questions about his abilities, 182
  racism encountered, 182–83
  statistics, 186
  Toronto FC, 183
  U.S. national team, 181–82
  Villareal, 181
  youngest American to score a hat trick, 181
  youngest player to score a goal in MLS history, 180
Amarildo, 227–28
American Soccer League (ASL), 141
Andorinha, 36
Andrulis, Greg, 189
Arena, Bruce, 121, 122, 126, 137, 148, 150–51, 152, 162, 168, 173, 176, 177, 184
Argentina's political situation, 233
Argentine Primera, 114
Argentinos Juniors, 29–30
Arriola, Paul, 254–55
Arsenal, 22, 105
AS Cannes, 66
Asensio, Marco, 258–59
Aston Villa, 192
AZ, 182

B

Baggio, Roberto, 240
Bahr, Walter, 142, 143, 144
Banks, Gordon, 214
Baresi, Franco, 82–83
Barthez, Fabien, 134
Basque independence movement, 107
Bayer Leverkusen, 120–21, 150
Bayern Munich, 45–46, 49, 108–09, 124
Beasley, DaMarcus, 122, 151
Beckenbauer, Franz
  1966 World Cup, 46
  1970 World Cup, 46, 230
  1974 World Cup, 46–47
  1990 World Cup, 49, 237
  2006 World Cup organizingcommittee, 49

Bayern Munich, 45–46, 49, 109
  coaching career, 48–49
  defensive skills, 44–45
  greatest German player ever, 44
  inspired by the 1954 World Cup, 45, 225
  New York Cosmos, 47–48
  North American Soccer League (NASL), 16–17
  playing style, 46–47
  statistics, 50
  West German national team coach, 48–49
Beckham, David, 112, 124, 241
betting on sports, 90
Blackburn, 105, 190
Boca Juniors, 29–30
Bocanegra, Carlos, 132
Bordeaux, 66
Borghi, Frank, 143–44
Borussia Mönchengladbach, 174–75
Bradley, Bob, 136, 171–75
Bradley, Michael
  2010 World Cup, 174
  2014 World Cup, 175–76
  2017 Gold Cup, 177
  2018 World Cup, 176–77
  Aston Villa, 175
  Borussia Mönchengladbach, 174–75
  Heerenveen, 173
  influenced by his father's role as coach, 171–75
  Serie A, 175
  statistics, 177–78
  and Tim Howard, 130
  Toronto FC, 176
Brasileiro Serie A, 114
Brazil
  country's debate over the best players of all time, 73–74, 227–28
  economic concerns, 246–47
  "Maracanazo" defeat, 223–24, 267
Brito, Waldemar de, 12
Brookhattan, 141
Buffon, Gianluigi
  1996 Olympics, 90
  2002 World Cup, 91
  2004 European Championship, 91
  2006 World Cup, 91–92, 213–14
  2010 World Cup, 92
  2018 World Cup, 92
  betting controversy, 90
  family of athletes, 88
  goalkeeping abilities, 87–88
  Juventus, 87–88, 89–90
  Parma, 87–88, 89
  retirement plans, 92–93
  and Ronaldo, 79
  statistics, 93

"Superman" nickname, 89
Bundesliga, 107–09

C

Cal FC, 160
Caligiuri, Paul
  1990 World Cup, 196–98, 199
  1994 World Cup, 199–200
  coaching career, 200
  college career, 195
  Columbus Crew, 200
  FC Hansa Rostock, 196
  first American to sign with the
    Bundesliga, 196
  Hamburger SV, 196
  Los Angeles Galaxy, 200
  pivotal moment in World Cup
    qualifying match, 197–98,
    200–01
  role in launching soccer within
    the U.S., 195, 198, 200–01
  Rose Bowl exhibition, 195–96
  statistics, 201
Calloway, Laurie, 157, 159
Cantona, Eric, 58–59
Carroll, Roy, 134
Carter-Vickers, Cameron, 255–56
Casillas, Iker, 95, 211–12
Catalonia's independence
  movement, 55, 107
Catenaccio style of defense, 80
Charlton, Sir Bobby, 11, 44–45, 229
Chelsea, 105
Chicago Fire, 172
Chicharito, 176–77
Chitalu, Godfrey, 249
Colombo, Charlie, 143–44
Columbus Crew, 189, 200
CONCACAF, 126
Confederations Cup (2009), 135,
  166
Copa América (2016), 26
Cruyff, Johan
  1974 World Cup, 47, 61, 98,
    231–33
  Ajax, 59–60, 63
  career highlights, 60
  coaching career, 63
  Cruyff Turn, 62
  FC Barcelona, 60, 63
  legacy of, 63–64
  Netherlands national team, 61
  North American Soccer League
    (NASL), 62–63
  rebellious nature of, 61–62, 232
  retirement and return to soccer,
    62–63, 233
  statistics, 64
  Total Football concept, 58, 60,
    231–32
Cruzeiro, 74–75

D

Daei, Ali, 249
defense, Catenaccio style, 80
Dembele, Ousmane, 257–58
Dempsey, Clint
  2006 World Cup, 165
  2009 Confederations Cup, 166
  2010 World Cup, 94, 125, 166–67
  2014 World Cup, 167

all-time goal scorer record,
  127, 162
American style of play, 162
college career, 164
financial struggles of his family,
  163–64
Fulham, 166
irregular heartbeat, 168
and Jozy Altidore, 184
and Landon Donovan, 167, 169
Major League Soccer (MLS)
  draft, 165
New England Revolution,
  165–66
played in adult leagues as a
  child, 163
Premier League record, 166
Seattle Sounders, 168
statistics, 170
Tottenham Hotspur, 167–68
toughness of, 169
unpredictability of, 167
Dempsey, Jennifer, 163–64
Dempsey, Ryan, 164
"designated player" rule, 112
Diop, Papa Bouba, 26
Donnarumma, Gianluigi, 262
Donovan, Landon
  2002 World Cup, 122–23, 211, 243
  2006 World Cup, 124
  2010 World Cup, 94, 124–26, 245
  2014 World Cup, 126–27, 167
  ability to play multiple
    positions, 121
  Bayer Leverkusen, 120–21, 123
  Bayern Munich, 124
  best U.S. player ever, 119–20,
    127–28
  childhood, 120
  and Clint Dempsey, 167, 169
  Everton, 124, 126
  Los Angeles Galaxy, 123–24, 126
  retirement, 127
  rhythm of the game, 148
  San Jose Earthquakes, 121, 123
  statistics, 128
  and Tim Howard, 119–20, 136
  U.S. national team, 122, 124–25
Dortmund, 205–06
drug problems, 33, 240
Duvalier, François, 145

E

English Football Association
  (FA), 4
English Premier League (EPL),
  104–06
Eredivisie, 113
Escobar, Andrés, 239, 266–67
Etoile Haitienne, 140–41
European Championship
  1964, 54
  2000, 68, 83, 91
  2004, 91
  2008, 51–52, 54
  2010, 55
  2012, 51–52, 92
  2016, 40–41, 92
Eusébio, 36
Everton, 124, 126, 134–35, 137

F

Fabregas, Cesc, 96
FC Barcelona, 21, 30–31, 52–53, 56,
  60, 63, 76, 106–07
FC Hansa Rostock, 196
FC Saarbrücken, 157
Fédération Internationale de
  Football Association (FIFA), 4,
  198, 238
Ferguson, Sir Alex, 37, 80, 134
Figo, Luis, 204
France's success with "Zizou,"
  67–68
Franco, Francisco, 107
French Ligue 1, 113
Friedel, Brad
  1998 World Cup, 189–90
  2002 World Cup, 190–91
  Aston Villa, 192
  Blackburn, 190
  coaching career, 192
  college career, 188
  Columbus Crew, 189
  desire to play overseas, 188–90
  Liverpool, 189, 190
  multisport athlete, 187–88
  Nottingham Forest, 188
  record for most consecutive
    Premier League games, 192
  statistics, 193
  Tottenham Hotspur, 192
  U.S. national team, 189–90
Fulham, 166
Furman University, 164

G

Gaetjens, Joe
  1950 World Cup, 141–44, 268
  childhood, 140
  Etoile Haitienne, 140–41
  Racing Club de France, 145
  return to Haiti, 145
  statistics, 146
  U.S. national team, 141–44
Gansler, Bob, 197
Garrincha, 226, 227, 228
George Mason University, 203
Germany
  before and after reunification,
    108
  after World War II, 45, 225
  "fan miles," 243–44
  "the Miracle of Bern," 45, 225,
    264
Ghiggia, Alcides, 267
goalkeepers, best, 87, 129, 187
goal(s)
  "Goal of the Century," 32,
    99–100, 236
  top ten best goals in World Cup
    history, 94–100
  top ten highest goal scorers in
    international history, 249
Gold Cup (2017), 177, 184–85
"Golden Generation" of Spanish
  players, 51
Götze, Mario, 248
Green, Julian, 136–37, 175–76
Guardiola, Pep, 24, 52, 53, 64

H

Haiti
  charitable causes within, 185
  political situation, 145–46
Hamburger SV, 196
Harkes, John, 159, 201
Harrisburg Heat, 204
Heerenveen, 173
Heitinga, John, 96
Hernández, Joaquim, 52
Hidegkuti, Nándor, 213
history
  19th century England, 3–4
  ancient forms of soccer, 3
  English Football Association
    (FA), 4
  Fédération Internationale de
    Football Association (FIFA),
    4, 198, 238
  first international soccer game, 4
  first World Cup event, 218–20
  highlights of the first twenty
    World Cup events, 217–49
  the next generation of
    superstars, 253–62
  politics of the La Liga rivalry,
    107
  soccer players with other full-
    time jobs, 140, 141
  suspension of the World Cup for
    World War II, 139, 221–23
  of the term "soccer," 5–6
  top ten highest goal scorers
    internationally, 249
  U.S. lack of participation, 4–6
Hitler, Adolf, 222
Horvath, Ethan, 256
Howard, Tim
  2009 Confederations Cup, 135
  2010 World Cup, 94, 125, 135–36
  2014 World Cup, 136–37, 209–10
  childhood, 130
  Everton, 134–35, 137
  goalkeeping abilities, 129
  injuries, 137
  The Keeper (Howard), 131
  and Landon Donovan, 119–20,
    136
  Manchester United (Man U),
    134–35
  and Michael Bradley, 130
  mistakes made, 134
  New Jersey Imperials, 132
  New York/New Jersey
    MetroStars, 132–33
  statistics, 138
  Tourette syndrome (TS), 130–31,
    133
  U.S. national team, 135, 137
Hughes, Rob, 198
human growth hormone, 20–21
Hungary as a world power in
  soccer, 224–25
Hurst, Geoff, 97, 229
hyperactivity, 155

I

Ibrahimovic, Zlatan, 68
Iniesta, Andrés, 53, 96, 246
Inter Milan, 76, 110

Iranian-U.S. political hostilities,
  241
irregular heartbeat, 36–37, 168

J

Jairzinho, 74
Jeffrey, Bill, 142
jogo bonito ("beautiful game"), 99
Júnior, Vinícius, 260–61
Juventus, 66, 87–88, 89–90, 110

K

Kahn, Oliver, 211
Kaká, 110
Kamamoto, Kunishige, 249
Keane, Roy, 27
The Keeper (Howard), 131
Keller, Kasey, 135, 189
Klinsmann, Jürgen, 126–27, 136,
  168, 175, 176, 244, 247
Klose, Miroslav, 78, 249
Kompany, Vincent, 210

L

La Liga, 38–39, 106–07, 181
Landa, Honorino, 212
leagues
  Argentine Primera, 114
  Brasileiro Serie A, 114
  Bundesliga, 107–09
  English Premier League (EPL),
    104–06
  Eredivisie, 113
  French Ligue 1, 113
  La Liga, 38–39, 106–07, 181
  Liga MX, 113
  Major League Soccer (MLS),
    110–13, 158–59, 165, 238
  North American Soccer League
    (NASL), 16–17, 111, 194–95
  Primeira Liga, 113
  relegation and promotion
    system, 104
  Serie A, 89, 109–10
Leicester City, 105
Leonardo, 239
Lewis, Eddie, 123
Liga MX, 113
Lineker, Gary, 32
Liverpool, 189, 190
Lloyd, Carli, 97
Los Angeles Galaxy, 112, 123–24,
  200
Lozano, Hirving, 261–62
Lukaku, Romelu, 210

M

Magath, Felix, 196
Major League Soccer (MLS),
  110–13, 158–59, 165, 238
Maldini, Cesare, 81–82
Maldini, Christian, 85–86
Maldini, Daniel, 85–86
Maldini, Paolo
  1990 World Cup, 82
  1994 World Cup, 82–83
  1998 World Cup, 83
  2002 World Cup, 83
  AC Milan, 84, 110
  awards and honors, 84–85
  defensive skills, 80–81

Italian national team, 82
Italy's most capped player, 83–84
  retirement, 84–85
  statistics, 86
  tennis career, 85
Manchester City, 105
Manchester United (Man U), 37,
  105–06, 134–35
"Maracanazo" defeat at the 1950
  World Cup, 223–24, 267
Maradona, Diego
  1982 World Cup, 30–31, 234
  1986 World Cup, 31–32, 99–100,
    235–36
  1990 World Cup, 32–33, 82, 265
  1994 World Cup, 33, 239–40
  Argentine national team, 29,
    233–34
  Argentinos Juniors, 29–30
  Boca Juniors, 29–30
  coaching career, 33–34
  compared to Lionel Messi, 28,
    33–34
  controversies about, 30, 31,
    33–34, 233–34
  drug problems, 33, 240
  FC Barcelona, 30–31
  "Goal of the Century," 32,
    99–100, 236
  Napoli, 31
  statistics, 34
Marseille, 49
Marzolini, Silvio, 30
Materazzi, Marco, 69–70, 244
Maurice, Michael, 197–98
Mbappé, Kylian, 256–57
media, state-controlled, 220–21
Meola, Tony, 132, 189, 198
Messi, Lionel
  2006 World Cup, 23
  2008 Olympics, 23–24
  2010 World Cup, 25
  2014 World Cup, 25, 247–48
  2018 World Cup, 26
  as an Argentine playing for
    Spain, 21–23
  Ballon d'Or award, 24
  compared to Cristiano Ronaldo,
    24–25, 35, 38, 106
  compared to Diego Maradona,
    28, 33–34
  dribbling abilities, 24
  FC Barcelona, 21, 26
  physical size, 19–21
  statistics, 27
Michels, Rinus, 60, 61, 231
Milutinovic, Bora, 157
"the Miracle of Bern," 45, 225, 264
Modric, Luka, 71
Mortensen, Stan, 143
most World Cup championships
  by country, 115
Müeller, Gerd, 47, 230
Müller, Thomas, 109
Mulqueen, Tim, 131
Mussolini, Benito, 220

N

Napoli, 31
Navas, Keylor, 209

the Netherlands as a world soccer
power, 58, 61, 232
Neuer, Manuel, 87, 109, 209
Newell's Old Boys, 20–21
New England Revolution, 165–66
New Jersey Imperials, 132
New York Cosmos, 16–17, 47–48
New York/New Jersey MetroStars,
132–33, 172–73, 180
New York Red Bulls, 151, 180–81
the next generation of superstars,
253–62
Neymar, 211
N'Kono, Thomas, 89
North American Soccer League
(NASL), 16–17, 111, 194–95
Nottingham Forest, 188

O
Ochoa, Guillermo, 211
Olympics
1972, 232
2008, 23–24, 181

P
Pak Doo-ik, 265
Parma, 87–88, 89
Patenaude, Bert, 219
Pelé
1958 World Cup, 13–14, 99, 226
1962 World Cup, 15, 227–28
1966 World Cup, 15, 228–29
1970 World Cup, 16, 98–99, 214,
229–31
awards and legendary status, 17
Brazilian national team, 13
Brazilian style to his game, 13
childhood, 11–12
greatest player ever, 11, 17–18,
226
New York Cosmos, 16–17, 48,
194–95
popularity worldwide, 14–15
Santos club, 12, 14–15, 17
statistics, 18, 249
Persie, Robin van, 95
Petit, Emmanuel, 97–98, 266
Phiri, Kinnah, 249
Piola, Silvio, 110
Platini, Michael, 235
popularity of soccer worldwide,
1–2, 6–7, 217–18, 229–30
Primeira Liga, 113
Pulisic, Christian
Dortmund, 205–06
family of soccer players, 203–04
first American soccer superstar,
202–03
popularity in Europe, 207–08
scoring abilities and skills, 207
sponsorship deals, 207
statistics, 208
U.S. national team, 206–08
youngest American in the
modern era to score, 206
Pulisic, Kelley, 203–04
Pulisic, Mark, 203–04, 208
Puskás, Ferenc, 225, 249
Puyol, Carlos, 19

R
racism, 182–83
Rahn, Helmut, 225, 264
Ramos, Tab, 197, 239, 267
Rangers, 150
Rashford, Marcus, 259–60
Real Madrid, 38–39, 70–71, 78,
106–07
Reschke, Michael, 120–21
Reyna, Claudio
1998 World Cup, 150
2002 World Cup, 150
2006 World Cup, 151
Bayer Leverkusen, 150
childhood dreams of the World
Cup, 149, 152
college career, 148–49
high school career, 148
injuries, 149, 150, 151
instinctive soccer abilities, 148
New York Red Bulls, 151
Rangers, 150
retirement and post-playing
career, 151–52
statistics, 153
U.S. national team, 149
Wolfsburg, 150
Reyna, Miguel, 147–48
Robben, Arjen, 212
Romario, 75
Ronaldinho, 22
Ronaldo
1996 Olympics, 75
1998 World Cup, 67, 76–77,
240–42, 266
2002 World Cup, 78, 243
2006 World Cup, 78
AC Milan, 78–79
childhood, 74
FC Barcelona, 76
FIFA Player of the Year, 76, 78
injuries, 75, 77–78, 79
Inter Milan, 76, 77
nicknames, 73–74, 75
PSV Eindhoven, 75
Real Madrid, 78
statistics, 79
and Zinedine Zidane ("Zizou"),
74
Ronaldo, Cristiano
2006 World Cup, 39–40, 244
2010 World Cup, 40
2014 World Cup, 40
2016 European Championship,
40–41
awards and achievements, 37
compared to Lionel Messi,
24–25, 35, 38, 106
compared to Ronaldo, 35–36
controversies about, 41–42
irregular heartbeat, 36–37
Manchester United, 37
popularity of, 41–42
Portuguese national team, 39–41
Real Madrid, 38–39
statistics, 42–43, 249
youth soccer experiences, 36–37
and Zinedine Zidane ("Zizou"),
71–72
Rooney, Wayne, 39–40

Rossi, Paolo, 210, 235
Ruiz, Bryan, 263

S
Saeed, Hussein, 249
San Diego Nomads, 195
San Diego State University, 156
San Francisco Bay Blackhawks, 157
San Jose Clash, 158–59, 160
San Jose Earthquakes, 121, 123
Santos club, 12, 14–15, 17
Sar, Edwin van der, 134
saves in World Cup history, top
ten, 209–14
Schmid, Sigi, 188, 191
Schweinsteiger, Bastian, 109
Seattle Sounders, 168
Senamuang, Kiatisuk, 249
Serie A, 89, 109–10
Shilton, Peter, 100
Silva, Leônidas da, 222
simplicity of the game, 2
South Africa as a new World Cup
venue, 245
Spain
"Barcelona style," 63
Basque independence
movement, 107
disappointing results, 53–54
divisions between Catalonia and
the rest of the country, 55, 107
La Liga rivalry, 106–07
"La Roja" team of 2008-2012, 55
"tiki-taka" philosophy, 51,
63, 246
Sparwasser, Jürgen, 264
sponsorship deals, 207, 232
Sporting CP, 36, 37
Stewart, Earnie, 267

T
Tardelli, Marco, 96
terrorism fears, 232
"tiki-taka" philosophy, 51, 63, 246
Toldo, Francesco, 91
top ten
best goals in World Cup history,
94–100
best saves in World Cup history,
209–14
biggest upsets in World Cup
history, 263–68
highest goal scorers in
international history, 249
Toronto FC, 176, 183
Total Football concept, 58, 60,
231–32
Tottenham Hotspur, 167–68, 192
Totti, Francesco, 110
Tourette syndrome (TS), 130–31,
133
Turek, Toni, 213

U
UCLA, 188, 195
Union of European Football
Associations (UEFA
championship, 103–04, 106
University of Virginia, 148–49
upsets in World Cup history, top
ten, 263–68

U.S. national team, 140, 141–44, 154, 159–60, 207–08
U.S. participation in soccer
  hosting the 1994 World Cup, 6, 111, 198–99, 237, 238–39
  Iranian-U.S. political hostilities, 241
  left out of the World Cup for many years, 194–95, 198–99
  Major League Soccer (MLS), 110–13, 238
  reasons for the delayed start, 4–6

V

Valdano, Jorge, 55
Villareal, 181

W

Weah, George, 253–54
Weah, Tim, 253–54
Williams, Bert, 143
Wolfsburg, 150
Woods, Chris, 136
World Cup
  1930, 218–20
  1934, 220–21
  1938, 221–22
  1950, 139–40, 141–44, 222–24, 267, 268
  1952, 213
  1954, 45, 224–25, 264
  1958, 13, 99, 226
  1962, 15, 212, 227–28
  1966, 15, 46, 97, 228–29, 265
  1970, 16, 46, 98–99, 214, 229–31
  1974, 47, 61, 98, 231–33, 263–64
  1978, 29, 61, 233–34
  1982, 30–31, 96, 210, 234–35
  1986, 31–32, 99–100, 235–36
  1990, 32–33, 49, 82, 156–57, 196–98, 199, 236–37, 264–65
  1994, 82–83, 157–58, 199–200, 238–40, 266–67
  1998, 67–68, 76–77, 83, 91, 97–98, 150, 159–60, 189–90, 240–42, 266
  2002, 68–69, 78, 83, 91, 122–23, 150, 190–91, 211, 242–43, 265–66
  2006, 23, 39–40, 49, 69–70, 78, 91–92, 124, 151, 165, 213–14
  2010, 25, 40, 51–52, 55, 92, 94, 95–96, 124–26, 135–36, 166–67, 174, 211–12, 245–46
  2014, 25, 40, 92, 95, 126–27, 136–37, 167, 175–76, 183–84, 209–10, 211, 246–48, 263
  2018, 26, 92, 176–77, 200, 248
  2022, 56, 248
  highlights of the first twenty, 217–48
  most championships by country, 115
  top ten best goals, 94–100
  top ten best saves, 209–14
  top ten biggest upsets, 263–68
  upcoming, 248
World War II and the suspension of the World Cup, 139, 221–23
Wynalda, Eric
  1990 World Cup, 156–57

1994 World Cup, 157–58
1998 World Cup, 159–60
all-time leading scorer record, 124, 154–55
attitude and temper problems, 156–57
broadcasting career, 160
coaching career, 160
college career, 156
FC Saarbrücken, 157
first significant goal scorer for the U.S., 154–55
hyperactivity, 155
role in Major League Soccer (MLS), 158–59, 160
San Francisco Bay Blackhawks, 157
San Jose Clash, 158–59, 160
statistics, 161

X

Xavi
  2008 European Championship, 54
  2010 European Championship, 55
  2010 World Cup, 55
  ability to unite Spain, 55
  Al Sadd, 56
  awards, 53, 54
  best player of the "Golden Generation," 51–52
  Champions League titles, 56
  FC Barcelona, 52–53, 56
  responsible for Spain's success, 53–54
  statistics, 56–57

Y

Yashin, Lev, 87, 212

Z

Zico, 210
Zidane, Smail, 65–66
Zidane, Zinedine ("Zizou")
  1998 World Cup, 67–68, 97–98, 241–42, 266
  2000 European Championship, 68
  2002 World Cup, 68–69
  2006 World Cup, 69–70, 213–14, 244–45
  Bordeaux, 66
  AS Cannes, 66
  childhood, 65–66
  coaching career, 71–72
  and Cristiano Ronaldo, 71–72
  emotional outbursts of, 66, 67, 69–70
  French national team, 67–69
  head-butting of Marco Materazzi, 69–70, 244–45
  Juventus, 66
  Real Madrid, 70–71
  and Ronaldo, 74
  statistics, 72
Zoff, Dino, 210

ANN KILLION has covered American sports for more than a quarter century. An award-winning columnist for the *San Francisco Chronicle,* she has covered several World Cups and pivotal moments in the rise of both American men's and women's soccer. She was named the 2014 California Sportswriter of the Year. She is a *New York Times* bestselling author, having co-written Solo: *A Memoir of Hope* with soccer star Hope Solo. She also coauthored *Throw Like a Girl* with softball great Jennie Finch. She is the author of *Champions of Women's Soccer.* She has two children and lives in Mill Valley, California.

Follow Ann on Twitter @annkillion

ALSO BY
ANN KILLION

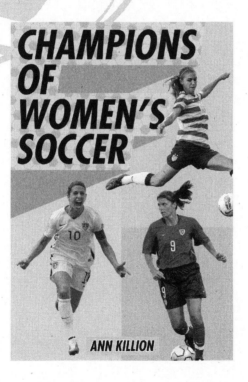